THE ART OF KOREAN COOKING

by
HARRIETT MORRIS

illustrations by
JOON LEE

CHARLES E. TUTTLE COMPANY
Rutland, Vermont: Tokyo, Japan

Representatives
Continental Europe: BOXERBOOKS, INC., Zurich
British Isles: PRENTICE-HALL INTERNATIONAL, INC., London
Australasia: BOOK WISE (AUSTRALIA) PTY. LTD.
104-108 Sussex Street, Sydney 2000

Published by the Charles E. Tuttle Company, Inc.,
of Rutland, Vermont and Tokyo, Japan,
with editorial offices at
Suido 1-chome, 2-6, Bunkyo-ku, Tokyo

Library of Congress Catalog
Card No. 59-10408

International Standard Book No. 0-8048-0036-7

First printing, 1959
Seventeenth printing, 1983

Printed in Japan

TABLE OF CONTENTS

KEEM-CHEE   23

SOUPS ✓   29

VEGETABLES   47

MEAT AND FOWL /

SEA FOOD 85

DESSERTS 91

MENU SUGGESTIONS   99

FOREWORD

The Art of Korean Cooking is a revised and enlarged edition of an earlier book, *Korean Recipes,* now out of print, which was begun in 1943 with extensive experimentation, in Wichita, Kansas, in order to make the recipes better adapted to western taste, and to include ingredients which, with little effort could be procured in most western cities.

The earlier book has had three private printings and has been widely distributed in many parts of the world. The purpose, at that time, was to introduce Korean foods to the Western world, and to provide scholarships by which Korean teachers and students could continue study abroad.

Korean food has for years been considered extremely delicious by those to whom it has been available. The preparation is time consuming, but there is a certain satisfaction that results from serving many dishes to your guests from which they may choose. Although they are highly seasoned when prepared by Korean housewives, the recipes in the present book have been modified considerably to suit the Western palate.

For many years the author has been revising and modifying the recipes through experimentation. In this she has been greatly assisted by Miss Sin Young Pang, formerly of the Ewha Woman's University faculty. The illustrations are by Mr. Joon Lee, also of Ewha University.

With the increase of general interest in Korea, and in all types of Oriental food, the author hopes this new and enlarged edition of her previously published book will find wide circulation. She anticipates that, with its publication by the Charles E. Tuttle Company, the enjoyment of Korean food will not be limited, but will be shared by folks in many lands.

July, 1959

Marion L. Conrow
Seoul, Korea

AUTHOR'S NOTE

Unless noted otherwise, all recipes in this book are for
6 servings.

The following instructions are frequently used in con-
nection with the recipes in this book and are gathered
together here to avoid repetition. Many recipes call for
a decoration of egg, some for prepared sesame seed; and
all the fried foods have their flavor further enhanced by
a dip into the vinegar-soy sauce. Directions for sprouting
beans at home are also given as bean sprouts are used
with a great variety of dishes.

EGG DECORATION

Separate the egg whites and yolks. Beat each slightly with
a fork. Cook by rolling a small amount of the egg into a
thin layer over the bottom of an oiled, heated skillet.
When firm, turn and cook lightly on the other side. Prepare the yolk in the same way. Use in recipes as directed.

PREPARED SESAME SEED

1 cup white sesame seed   1 tsp. salt

Remove any sand found among the seeds. Wash, if necessary. Put in a heavy skillet and brown slowly, stirring
constantly. When the seeds are brown and rounded, remove at once from the fire. Add salt. Mash the seeds until
pulverized. Sesame seed is used in this form in most recipes.

VINEGAR-SOY SAUCE

| 6 tbsp. soy sauce | 2 tbsp. sugar |
| 6 tbsp. vinegar | 1 tbsp. chopped pine nuts |

Combine soy sauce, vinegar, and sugar. Mix well and put 2 tbsp. of the sauce into individual dishes. Chop the pine nuts into fine pieces. Sprinkle over the top of each dish of soy sauce. The vinegar-soy sauce is served individually because all fried foods are dipped into it before they are eaten.

DIRECTIONS FOR SPROUTING BEANS

Bean sprouts may be grown from 2 kinds of beans, the small green Chinese mung bean, or the larger yellow soy bean. 1 cup of dry beans will yield approximately 2–3 cups of sprouts. Beans that are old will not sprout well.

Look over beans and remove any that are cracked or broken as these will not sprout. Wash beans well, put into a 2-quart large-mouthed jar and soak 12 hours.

Pour off water. Place jar on its side. Raise the bottom of the jar several inches so that all the water can drain off. Keep in this position until beans are sprouted.

3 times a day pour lukewarm water over the beans and drain. The beans should be kept damp but not wet. At night, add a pinch of chlorinated lime to the water used to rinse the beans. Keep the jar in a dark place where air circulates freely.

Sprouting time depends upon the temperature. In cooler weather 3–5 days are sufficient. When sprouts have formed, wash well and remove the skins from the beans, also the hairlike end from each sprout. Use in recipes as directed.

CEREALS

Even though a man has three feet of beard, if he has nothing to eat, he is not a gentleman. (KOREAN PROVERB)

Rice is the most commonly used grain in Korea, and is served at practically every meal. It is usually prepared plain without the addition of salt. Sometimes other grains, beans, vegetables, or fruits are cooked with the rice.

WHITE RICE
(Heen pahb)

    2 cups white rice
    2½ cups cold water

Pick over the rice carefully and wash 5 times. Add the cold water to the rice, cover tightly, and bring quickly to a boil. Reduce the heat as low as possible and steam 30 minutes. Do not stir or remove the lid while the rice is cooking. The grains of rice will be separate and distinct when prepared in this way.

RICE WATER
(Soong-nyung)

After the rice has been removed from the kettle, there is always some that adheres to the bottom of the pan. Add several cups of water, bring quickly to a boil, and serve hot.

RICE AND BEAN SPROUTS NO. 1
(Kong na-mool pahb) No. 1

    2 cups rice
    ¾ cup prepared bean
      sprouts
    2½ cups cold water
    1 tsp. salt

Place bean sprouts on the bottom of a heavy kettle. Pick over the rice, wash 5 times, and put it on top of the bean sprouts. Add salt and cold water, cover tightly, and bring quickly to a boil. Reduce the heat as low as possible and steam 30 minutes. Do not stir or remove the lid while cooking.

RICE AND BEAN SPROUTS NO. 2
(Kong na-mool pahb) No. 2

2 cups rice
3 cups cold water
1 cup prepared bean sprouts
1 green onion

1 clove garlic
2 tsp. prepared sesame seed (see recipe p. 11)
2 tbsp. soy sauce
1 tsp. oil

Pick over the rice carefully, wash 5 times, and add the cold water. Combine chopped green onion (including top), chopped garlic, prepared sesame seed, soy sauce, oil, and bean sprouts; cook all together for 2 minutes, stirring well. Combine bean sprout mixture and rice, cover tightly, and bring quickly to a boil. Reduce the heat as low as possible and steam 30 minutes. Do not stir or remove the lid while cooking.

RICE AND BEANS
(Paht pahb)

2 cups rice
½ cup red beans
3 cups cold water

Wash the beans well, cover with water, and let stand 2 hours. Cook until tender. Drain water from the beans and save it. Pick over the rice, wash 5 times, and add it to the beans. To the water drained from the beans, add extra water to make up 3 cups. Add to the rice and beans. Cover tightly and bring quickly to a boil. Reduce the heat as low as possible and steam 30 minutes. Do not stir or remove the lid while cooking.

RICE AND MUSHROOMS

(Song-i pahb)

2 cups rice
1 cup sliced mushrooms
1 cup sliced onions
½ cup chopped lean beef
2 tbsp. soy sauce
speck pepper
1 tbsp. oil
2 tsp. prepared sesame seed (see recipe p. 11)
3 cups cold water
½ tsp. salt

Pick over the rice carefully and wash 5 times. Slice mushrooms and onions in thin slices. Chop or grind beef fine. Add to the mushrooms and onions, then add soy sauce, pepper, oil, and prepared sesame seed. Mix together. Cook for 2 minutes, stirring well. Add meat mixture to the rice. Add cold water and salt. Cover tightly and bring quickly to a boil. Reduce heat as low as possible and steam 30 minutes. Do not stir or remove the lid while cooking.

RICE AND POTATOES

(Kahm-cha pahb)

2 cups rice	3 cups cold water
1 cup diced potato	1 tsp. salt

Pick over the rice carefully and wash 5 times. Peel the potato and dice into ½-inch pieces. Add to the rice. Add cold water and salt. Cover tightly and bring quickly to a boil. Reduce the heat as low as possible and steam 30 minutes. Do not stir or remove the lid while cooking.

(Pi-bium pahb)

4 cups rice	6 tbsp. soy sauce
5 cups cold water	2 cups shredded celery
½ lb. beef	salt
3 green onions	1 carrot
1½ cloves garlic	2 cucumbers
speck pepper	2 cups prepared bean
3 tbsp. prepared sesame	sprouts
seed (see recipe p. 11)	2 eggs
3 tsp. oil	1 firm pear

Pick over the rice and wash 5 times. Add cold water, cover tightly, and bring quickly to a boil. Reduce the heat as low as possible and steam 30 minutes. Do not stir or remove the lid while cooking.

Chop or grind the beef into fine pieces. Chop finely 2 green onions (including tops), and 1 clove garlic. Add to the beef. Add pepper, 2 tbsp. prepared sesame seed, 1 tsp. oil, and 4 tbsp. soy sauce. Mix well. Cook slowly until the meat is done, stirring constantly.

Wash the celery and cut into 1-inch lengths. Shred each piece lengthwise. Sprinkle with salt and let stand 10 minutes. Press out any water that forms and fry the celery in ½ tsp. oil for 2 minutes.

Wash the cucumber. Without peeling it, cut into 1-inch lengths and shred each piece lengthwise. Sprinkle with salt and let stand 10 minutes. Press out any water that forms and fry in ½ tsp. oil for 2 minutes.

Wash and peel the carrot. Cut into 1-inch lengths and shred each piece lengthwise. Cook for 3 minutes in boiling, salted water. Drain.

If fresh bean sprouts are used, prepare them by removing the skins of the beans and the hairlike end on each sprout. Wash and cook in hot water until tender. Drain. If canned bean sprouts are used, drain well. To the bean sprouts, add 2 tbsp. soy sauce, 1 chopped green onion (including top), ½ clove chopped garlic, 1 tsp. oil, and 1 tbsp. prepared sesame seed. Mix well and cook until seasonings are all absorbed.

Use 2 eggs. To decorate, see recipe for egg decoration on page 11. When prepared, roll each layer separately into a long tube-shape and shred crosswise as thinly as possible.

Peel the pear and shred in strips about 1 inch long.

Put aside the pear, egg, cucumber and ½ of the carrot. Add other prepared foods to the rice, mixing lightly.

Serve in bowls or on plates. Decorate the top with the pear, egg, cucumber, and carrot. This recipe provides for 10–12 servings.

RICE AND BEAN "JOOK"

(Paht-jook)

1 cup red beans	11 cups water
1 cup rice	2 tsp. salt

Wash the beans well. Add 6 cups of water and soak overnight. Add 1 tsp. salt and cook until tender about 2 hours. Mash and run through a coarse strainer.

Wash rice 5 times. Add 1 tsp. salt and 2 cups cold water. Bring quickly to a boil. Reduce the heat as low as possible and steam 30 minutes.

Combine the rice and beans. Add 3 cups hot water and cook until well done and of the consistency of breakfast cereal. Stir often to prevent burning.

Dumplings

6 tbsp. flour	½ tsp. salt
½ tsp. baking powder	water

Sift flour, baking powder and salt together. Add enough cold water to make a stiff dough. Knead well and make into balls ¼ inch in diameter. Before serving, add the dumplings, cover, and cook slowly 10 minutes.

WHEAT FLOUR NOODLES

(Mill-kook-soo)

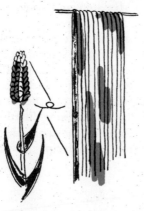

Soup

¼ lb. beef
2 green onions
1 clove garlic
4 tbsp. soy sauce
1 tbsp prepared sesame
    seed (see recipe p. 11)
speck pepper
1 tsp. oil
6 cups hot water
2 eggs

Cut the beef into thin slices 1 inch square. Add 1 chopped onion (including top), chopped garlic, soy sauce, prepared sesame seed, pepper, and oil. Mix well and cook until the beef is well seared. Add hot water and boil until the meat is tender. When almost done, add the remaining green onion, including the top, cut into pieces 1½ inches long and shred lengthwise.

Use two eggs. To prepare for decoration see recipe for egg decoration on page 11. When prepared, roll each layer separately into a long tube shape and shred crosswise as thinly as possible.

Noodles

3 cups flour
1 egg
2 tsp. salt
¾ cup water

Mix flour and salt. Add unbeaten egg and enough water (about ¾ cup) to make a stiff dough. Knead the mixture for 15–20 minutes, and roll out to ⅛-inch in thickness. Sprinkle with flour and cut into ⅛-inch strips. Put the noodles in rapidly boiling water, stirring enough to keep them from sticking together, and cook 10–15 minutes. Remove. Wash in cold water and drain well.

Put noodles in individual bowls and cover with the boiling hot soup. Decorate the top of each bowl with white and yellow strips of egg and shredded red chile pepper, if desired.

RICE AND SWEET POTATOES
(Ko-koo-mah pahb)

  2 cups rice
  1 cup diced sweet potato
  ½ cup green peas or
     fresh soybeans
  3 cups cold water

Peel and cut the sweet potato into ½-inch cubes. Pick over the rice, wash 5 times. Add peas or soybeans, sweet potato, and cold water. Cover tightly and bring quickly to a boil. Reduce the heat as low as possible and steam 30 minutes. Do not stir or remove the lid while cooking.

RICE AND BARLEY
(Po-ri pahb)

  1½ cups rice
  ½ cup pearled barley
  4 cups water

Add 2 cups boiling water to the barley and soak for 12 hours. Cook ½ hour. Pick over the rice and wash 5 times. Combine the rice and barley. Add 2 cups cold water. Cover tightly and bring quickly to a boil. Reduce the heat as low as possible and steam 30 minutes. Do not stir or remove the lid while cooking.

RICE AND GREEN PEAS

(Kong pahb)

   2 cups rice
   ½ cup green peas
   3 cups cold water

Wash and shell peas. Wash the rice well. Add the water and bring rice quickly to a boil. Boil for 8 minutes. Add green peas. Reduce the heat as low as possible and steam for 15 minutes. The peas will be on top of the rice. When serving, mix peas and rice together.

RICE AND CHESTNUTS

(Palm pahb)

   2 cups rice
   1 cup prepared chestnuts
   3½ cups water

Peel the chestnuts and cut into halves. Wash rice well. Combine rice and chestnuts, add water, and bring quickly to a boil. Reduce the heat as low as possible and steam 30 minutes. Do not stir or remove the lid while rice is cooking.

RICE AND DATES

(Tai-chooh pahb)

   2 cups rice
   ½ cup seeded dates
   2¾ cups cold water

Pick over the rice carefully, wash 5 times and add cold water. Remove the seeds from the dates and quarter. Add dates to the rice, cover tightly, and bring quickly to a boil. Reduce the heat as low as possible and steam 30 minutes. Do not stir or remove the lid while cooking.

KEEM-CHEE

Small, but nevertheless a pepper seed. (KOREAN PROVERB)

Keem-chee is a pickle that is served at practically all meals. It is made from raw vegetables and is a good source of vitamins.

TURNIP "KEEM-CHEE"

(Moo keem-chee)

> 6 medium turnips
> 1 red chile pepper
> 1½ tbsp. salt
> 1 tsp. candied ginger
> 1½ cups water

Wash, peel, and quarter turnips. Add 1 tbsp. salt and let stand 2 days. Save the salt water that forms on the turnips. Remove the turnips and slice in pieces ¼ inch in thickness. Put the turnips in a jar. Add chopped ginger, chopped red pepper, ½ tbsp. salt, and the salt water from the turnips, plus enough extra water to make 1½ cups. Mix well and put in refrigerator for 2 weeks. Serve the water with the turnips.

CUCUMBER "KEEM-CHEE"

(O-i keem-chee)

> 3 large cucumbers
> 1½ tbsp. salt
> 1 green onion
> ½ clove garlic
> ½ tsp. chopped red chile pepper
> ½ cup of water

Wash the cucumbers and, without peeling, cut them into 1½-inch lengths. Cut each piece in half lengthwise and remove the seeds. Add 1 tbsp. salt to the cucumbers. Mix well and let stand 15 minutes.

Cut the onion (including top) into 1½-inch lengths and shred each piece lengthwise very finely.

Chop the garlic and red chile pepper into fine pieces.

Wash the salt from the cucumbers. Add onion, garlic, red pepper, ½ tbsp. salt, and water. Mix well. Set aside to ripen. In warm weather 2 days are sufficient, but in cold weather 1 week is required.

WINTER "KEEM-CHEE"

(Tong keem-chee)

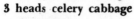

3 heads celery cabbage
¾ cup salt
8 turnips
6 cloves garlic
6 tbsp. chopped **red** chile pepper
2 tsp. chopped **candied** ginger
2 green onions
2 stalks celery
¼ cup chestnuts
1 firm pear
water

Remove the outside leaves of the cabbage. Wash the leaves and also the heads of cabbage and place all in a large jar. Sprinkle with ½ cup of salt and let stand 3 hours.

Wash and peel turnips. Shred 1½ cups into fine strips 1 inch long and cut the remainder into thin slices. Combine the two. Add ¼ cup salt and let stand 30 minutes. Drain. Remove the sliced turnip. To the shredded turnip, add the chopped garlic, chopped red peppers, and chopped ginger. Cut the green onions (including tops) into 1½-inch lengths, shred lengthwise, and add to the turnip mixture. Mix well.

Wash and cut celery into 1½-inch lengths and shred lengthwise.

Peel chestnuts and cut into fine pieces. Wash and peel pear and shred in fine pieces. Add celery, chestnuts and pear to turnip mixture.

Remove heads of cabbage from the brine. Wash well and drain. Open the leaves of cabbage without breaking them and pack the turnip mixture down in between each leaf.

Fold leaves back in place. Wrap some of the longer outside leaves around the top of the cabbage head to keep the turnip mixture from coming out. Put cabbage heads into a large jar. Add sliced turnip and cover with the outer leaves of cabbage that have been in the brine. Cover and place a weight on the cabbage. Let stand 2 days. Make a brine of 4 cups water to ¾ cup of salt and cover the cabbage heads, not including the outer leaves on top. Cover the jar and let stand 1 month. When serving, remove head from the brine and cut into circles 2 inches thick, crosswise. Place the cut side up in the dish in which it is served. For 25 to 30 servings.

SPRING "KEEM-CHEE"

(Pom keem-chee)

3 cups celery cabbage	½ tsp. chopped red chile pepper
3 tbsp. salt	
3 green onions	1 tsp. chopped candied ginger
1 clove garlic	
	1½ cups water

Wash the cabbage and cut into pieces 1 inch long and 1 inch wide. Sprinkle with 2 tbsp. salt. Mix well and let stand 15 minutes. Cut the onions (including tops) into 1½-inch lengths and shred lengthwise.

Chop the garlic, red pepper and ginger in fine pieces. After the cabbage has stood 15 minutes, wash it twice in cold water. Mix the prepared vegetables with the cabbage. Add 1 tbsp. salt and put into a stone or glass jar. Add enough water to cover the cabbage and let stand for several days. In warm weather, 1 day is sufficient, but in cold weather 5 days are needed. *Keem-chee* can be kept several weeks in the refrigerator.

"KEEM-CHEE" IN SOY SAUCE

(Jahng keem-chee)

3 heads celery cabbage	1 tbsp. salt
1 cup sliced turnip	4 green onions
1 cucumber	¼ cup shredded celery
1¼ cups soy sauce	1 firm pear
3 cloves garlic	6 chestnuts
1 tsp. candied ginger	6 dates
1 tbsp. chopped chile pepper	¼ cup pine nuts
	1/3 cup sugar

Wash the cabbage heads. Carefully remove the outside leaves and place them in a stone jar. Separate the tender inside leaves and cut into pieces 1½-inches square. Put them into the stone jar. Add ¼ cup soy sauce. Mix well. Let stand 3 hours, or until cabbage is soft. Stir several times so that cabbage will be flavoured with the soy sauce.

Wash, peel turnips, and cut into very thin slices. Wash cucumber and, without peeling it, cut lengthwise, remove the seeds, and slice in thin slices crosswise. Combine the turnips and cucumber and ¼ cup soy sauce. Mix well. Let stand 3 hours, or until soft. Stir occasionally.

Drain the soy sauce from the cabbage, turnips and cucumber, and save it. Mix vegetables and 1 tbsp. salt.

Chop garlic, ginger, peppers, onions (including tops), and add to the cabbage mixture. Cut celery into 1½-inch lengths. Shred fine lengthwise and add to the cabbage. Peel and slice pear in flat pieces 1 inch square. Peel chestnuts and slice thin. Remove seeds from dates and quarter. Add pear, chestnuts, dates, and pine-nuts to the cabbage mixture. Mix well. Remove large leaves from the stone jar and put in the cabbage mixture. Add sugar and enough of the saved soy sauce (in the proportion of 2 cups water to ½ cup soy sauce) to cover vegetables.

Cover the top of the *keem-chee* with the large leaves that were soaked in the soy sauce. Let stand 2–3 weeks.

SOUPS

One cannot distinguish the flavor of boiling soup.

(KOREAN PROVERB)

Rich delicious soups are served in Korea. They are almost always served hot and constitute an important part of the meal.

SPINACH SOUP
(See-kum-chee kook)

¼ lb. beef	1 tsp. salt
2 green onions	speck pepper
1 clove garlic	6 cups fresh spinach
1 tbsp. prepared sesame	(1 lb.)
seed (see recipe p. 11)	7 cups water
4 tbsp. soy sauce	

Cut beef into thin slices 1 inch square. Add chopped onions (including tops), chopped garlic, prepared sesame seed, soy sauce, salt and pepper. Mix well. Cook for a few minutes, until meat is well seared. Add water and cook until the meat is tender. Wash spinach well. Just before serving the soup, add spinach and cook only until it is tender.

MUSHROOM SOUP
(Puh-sut kook)

¼ lb. beef	speck pepper
4 tbsp. soy sauce	1 cup sliced mushrooms
2 green onions	1 large carrot
1 clove garlic	7 cups water
1 tbsp. prepared sesame	salt
seed (see recipe p. 11)	

Cut beef into thin slices 1 inch square. Add 2 tbsp. soy sauce, onions (including tops), which have been cut diagonally into ½-inch lengths, chopped garlic, prepared sesame seed, and pepper. Mix well. Slice mushrooms and add to the meat. Wash and scrape carrot. Notch lengthwise every ⅛ inch around the carrot and cut crosswise in thin flower-like circles. Add to the meat and cook until meat is well seared. Add water and remaining 2 tbsp. soy sauce and cook until tender. Season with salt.

BEAN SPROUT SOUP

(Kong na-mool kook)

¼ lb. beef	½ tbsp. prepared sesame
2 green onions	seed (see recipe p. 11)
1 clove garlic	4 tbsp. soy sauce
speck pepper	3 cups fresh or canned
salt	bean sprouts
	7 cups water

Cut beef into thin slices 1 inch square. Chop onion (reserving top) and garlic fine and add to the meat. Add pepper, prepared sesame seed, 2 tbsp. soy sauce. Mix together. Cook until the meat is well seared.

If fresh bean sprouts are used, prepare them by removing the hairlike end on each sprout. Wash well and add to the meat. If canned bean sprouts are used, drain, and add to the meat. Mix and cook 3 minutes.

Add water and 2 tbsp. soy sauce to the beef and sprouts and cook 30 minutes or until the sprouts and meat are tender. When almost done, cut the green tops of the onions in 2-inch lengths and add to the soup. Continue cooking 5 minutes. Season with salt.

CABBAGE SOUP

(Paj-hoo kook)

¼ lb. beef	3 cups celery cabbage
4 tbsp. soy sauce	1 onion
1 clove garlic	7 cups water
1 tbsp. prepared sesame	salt
seed (see recipe p. 11)	1 egg
speck pepper	

Cut the beef into thin slices 1 inch square. Add 2 tbsp. soy sauce, chopped garlic, prepared sesame seed, and pepper. Mix well. Cut celery cabbage into pieces 1 inch square, slice onions into thin slices and mix with the meat. Cook for 5 minutes, stirring constantly. Add water and remaining 2 tbsp. soy sauce and cook until meat and vegetables are tender. Season with salt. If desired, an egg may be stirred into the soup just before serving.

EGG PLANT SOUP

(Ka-gi kook)

- ¼ lb. beef
- 2 green onions
- 1 clove garlic
- 1 tbsp prepared sesame seed (see recipe p. 11)
- speck pepper
- 4 tbsp. soy sauce
- 7 cups water
- 1 medium egg plant
- 4 tbsp. flour
- 2 eggs
- 2 tbsp. oil
- 2 tsp. salt

Cut the beef into thin slices 1 inch square. Add chopped onions (including tops), chopped garlic, prepared sesame seed, pepper, and 2 tbsp. soy sauce. Mix well and cook until meat is well seared. Add water and remaining 2 tbsp. soy sauce and cook until meat is done.

Peel the egg plant, cut into pieces 2 inches long, 1 inch wide and ¼ inch thick. Roll each piece in flour, then in slightly beaten egg. Fry in a small amount of oil. Sprinkle with salt. When ready to serve the soup, add the eggplant and reheat. Season with salt, if necessary.

POTATO SOUP

(Kam-ja kook)

¼ lb. beef	speck pepper
3 green onions	7 cups water
4 tbsp. soy sauce	5 small potatoes
1 tbsp. prepared sesame seed (see recipe p. 11)	salt

Cut the beef into thin slices 1 inch square. Add chopped onions (reserving tops), soy sauce, prepared sesame seed, and pepper. Mix well. Cook until meat is well seared. Wash, peel, and cut potatoes into ½-inch cubes. Add to meat. Add water and cook until meat and potatoes are tender. When almost done, cut onion tops into 1½-inch lengths and add. Cook a few minutes longer and serve. Season with salt if necessary.

VEGETABLE SOUP

(Cha-soh kook)

¼ lb. beef	7 cups water
speck pepper	1½ cups celery cabbage
1 tbsp. prepared sesame seed (see recipe p. 11)	½ cup carrot
1 tsp. oil	1 small onion
4 tbsp. soy sauce	1 cup potatoes
	salt

Cut beef into thin slices 1 inch square. Add pepper, prepared sesame seed, oil, and soy sauce. Cook until the meat is well seared. Add water. Cut celery cabbage into pieces 1½ inch by 1 inch. Peel carrot and cut in 1 inch lengths, then slice each piece lengthwise in 3 or 4 flat pieces. Slice onions. Peel and slice potatoes into pieces 1½ inches long, 1 inch wide and ¼ inch thick. Add the vegetables to the soup and cook until tender. Season with salt. An egg may be stirred into soup before serving.

GREEN ONION SOUP

(Pah kook)

¼ lb. beef	1 tsp. oil
4 tbsp. soy sauce	7 cups water
1 tbsp prepared sesame seed (see recipe p. 11)	3 green onions (including tops)
1 clove garlic	1 egg
speck pepper	salt

Cut beef into thin slices 1 inch square. Add soy sauce prepared sesame seed, pepper, chopped garlic, and oil. Cook until meat is well seared. Add the water and cook until the meat is tender. Wash the onions and cut onions and tops into 2-inch lengths. When soup is almost done, add the onions and cook until tender. When ready to serve add slightly beaten egg to the soup and stir rapidly for one minute. Season with salt.

EGG SOUP

(Ke-ran kook)

¼ lb. beef	1 tbsp. oil
4 tbsp soy sauce	7 cups water
speck pepper	6 green onion tops
1 tbsp. prepared sesame seed (see recipe p. 11)	3 eggs
	salt

Cut beef into thin slices 1 inch square. Add 2 tbsp. soy sauce, pepper, prepared sesame seed, and oil. Cook until meat is well seared. Add water and remaining 2 tbsp. soy sauce. Cook until meat is almost tender. When almost done, cut onion tops into 1½-inch lengths, add to the soup, and cook until tender. Just before serving, add slightly beaten eggs all at once and stir. Serve immediately.

CUCUMBER SOUP

(O-i kook)

¼ lb. beef	speck pepper
4 tbsp. soy sauce	7 cups water
1 clove garlic	2 cups diced cucumber
1 tbsp. prepared sesame seed (see recipe p. 11)	1 medium onion
1 tsp. oil	1 egg
	salt

Cut beef into thin slices 1 inch square. Add 2 tbsp. soy sauce, chopped garlic, prepared sesame seed, oil and pepper. Cook together until the meat is well seared. Add the water and remaining 2 tbsp. soy sauce and cook until the meat is almost tender.

Wash cucumbers, but do not peel. Cut into halves lengthwise, remove seeds and cut into ½-inch pieces.

Wash onion and slice into thin pieces. Add cucumbers and onion to the soup, and cook until meat and vegetables are tender. Just before serving, add a slightly beaten egg to the soup and stir rapidly 1 minute. Season with salt.

FISH SOUP NO. 1

(Sang-suhn kook)

¼ lb. beef	7 cups water
4 tbsp. soy sauce	2 cups prepared bean sprouts
2 green onions	1 turnip
1 clove garlic	1 lb. cod fish
1 tbsp. prepared sesame seed (see recipe p. 11)	½ tsp. candied ginger
pepper	salt

Cut beef into thin slices 1 inch square. Add 2 tbsp. soy sauce, chopped onions, (including tops), chopped garlic, prepared sesame seed, and pepper. Cook until the meat is well seared. Add water and remaining 2 tbsp. sauce.

If fresh bean sprouts are used, prepare them by removing the hairlike end on each sprout. Wash well and add to the meat. If canned bean sprouts are used, drain and add to the meat. Wash, peel, and cut the turnip into thin slices 1 inch square and add to the meat. Cook until meat and vegetables are partially done.

Clean, skin, and bone the fish. Cut into pieces 2 inches square and add to soup. Chop candied ginger fine and add to soup. Season with salt and serve when fish is tender.

FISH SOUP NO. 2

(Sang-suhn kook)

¼ lb. beef
4 tbsp. soy sauce
2 green onions
1 clove garlic
½ tsp. candied ginger
speck pepper
7 cups water
1 lb. cod fish
3 tbsp. flour
2 eggs
2 tbsp. oil
salt
1 cup fresh spinach

Cut beef into thin slices 1 inch square. Add 2 tbsp. soy sauce, chopped onions (including tops), chopped garlic, chopped ginger, and pepper. Mix well. Cook until the meat is well seared. Add water and remaining 2 tbsp. soy sauce and cook until meat is tender.

Skin and bone the fish. Cut into pieces 2 inches square and ½ inch thick. Sprinkle with salt, roll in flour, then in slightly beaten egg, and fry in a small amount of oil. Wash and clean spinach. Add it together with the fish to the hot soup. Reheat. Season with salt.

OYSTER SOUP

(Gool kook)

7 cups water
3 cups oysters
salt
pepper
1/4 lb. beef
4 tbsp. soy sauce
1 tbsp. prepared sesame
seed (see recipe p. 11)
1 clove garlic

Cut beef into thin slices 1 inch square. Add 2 tbsp. soy sauce, prepared sesame seed, pepper, and chopped garlic. Cook until meat is well seared. Add water and remaining 2 tbsp. soy sauce. Cook until meat is tender. Remove any pieces of shell from the oysters and add to the hot soup. Reheat slowly until edges of oysters curl. Season with salt and serve at once.

CLAM SOUP
(Cho-kai kook)

1/4 lb. beef	1 clove garlic
4 tbsp. soy sauce	7 cups water
1 tbsp. prepared sesame seed (see recipe p. 11)	3 cups clams
speck pepper	salt

Cut the beef into thin slices 1 inch square. Add 2 tbsp. soy sauce, prepared sesame seed, pepper, and chopped garlic. Cook until the meat is tender. Clean fresh clams, or use canned clams. Add clams to the hot soup. Reheat slowly until clams are cooked. Season with salt and serve at once.

BEEF BALL SOUP

(Wan-ja kook)

½ lb. beef	speck pepper
¼ cup bean curd or cottage cheese	2 tbsp. oil
2 green onions	2 eggs
2 cloves garlic	2 tbsp. flour
2 tbsp. prepared sesame seed (see recipe p. 11)	2 tbsp. pine nuts
	½ cup sliced mushrooms
6 tbsp. soy sauce	7 cups water
	salt

Divide the meat into 2 parts. Chop or grind the most tender parts very fine. Press liquid from the bean curd or cottage cheese and add to the meat. Add 1 chopped onion (including top), 1 clove chopped garlic, 1 tbsp. prepared sesame seed, 2 tbsp. soy sauce, pepper, and 1 tbsp. oil. Mix well. Shape the meat into small balls ¼ inch in diameter enclosing 2 pine nuts in each ball. Roll each ball in flour then in slightly beaten egg and fry in a small amount of oil.

Cut the remaining meat into 1-inch cubes. Add 1 chopped green onion (reserving the top), 1 chopped clove garlic, 1 tbsp. prepared sesame seed, 2 tbsp. soy sauce, 1 tbsp. oil, speck of pepper, and mushrooms which have been sliced. Cook all together until the meat is well seared. Add water and 2 tbsp. soy sauce. Cook until the meat is tender. When almost done, add the onion tops cut into 1½ inch lengths. Cook until tender. Add meat balls and reheat slowly. Season with salt. Decorate the top of each bowl with egg.

Use 2 eggs. To prepare for decoration, see recipe on page 11. When prepared, cut into ½-inch diamond-shaped pieces and use both yellow and white as decoration for each bowl of soup.

SESAME SEED SOUP

(Cho-kay tang)

1 small chicken
1 tbsp. soy sauce
2 green onions
speck pepper
salt
¼ tsp. ginger root
2 cups sesame seed
3 cucumbers
oil
½ cup mushrooms
2 eggs
2 firm, hard pears
3 tbsp. pine nuts

Clean chicken. Cover with boiling water and cook whole until tender. Cut chicken from the bones in thin flat pieces 1½ inches long. Add soy sauce, chopped green onion (including top), pepper, salt, and chopped ginger root. Cool the chicken broth and remove all fat.

Wash the sesame seed. Cover with water and let stand 2 hours. Rub in the hands to remove the outside covering. Wash under water so the hull will come to the top. Drain seeds well. Put into a heavy skillet over a low fire and heat, stirring constantly, until seeds are well rounded. Do not brown the seeds. When well rounded, remove from the fire, add a little water, and mash the seed thoroughly. Water will form. Put all through a fine strainer. Combine this liquid with the chicken broth.

Cut unpeeled cucumbers lengthwise into thin flat pieces 1 inch long and ½ inch wide. Sprinkle with salt and let stand 5 minutes. Drain off any water that forms. Fry in a small amount of oil for a minute, or until a bright green color. Do not overcook.

Cut mushrooms in pieces the same size as the cucumber. Fry slightly in a small amount of oil.

To prepare eggs for decoration see recipe on page 11. When prepared cut into pieces same size as cucumber.

Wash and peel pear and cut in pieces the same size as cucumber. Place in salted water to keep the color from turning dark.

Mix together chicken, cucumber, mushrooms, egg and pear. To this add the sesame seed liquid. Serve cold in soup bowls. Add a few pine nuts to each bowl of soup.

BEEF AND TURNIP SOUP
(Ko-oum kook)

½ lb. beef
3 large turnips
8 cups water
3 green onions
1 tbsp. prepared sesame
 seed (see recipe p. 11)
3 tbsp. soy sauce
speck pepper
1 egg
salt

Cut the meat into 3 large pieces. Peel turnips and add whole to the meat. Add water and cook until meat and turnips are tender. Remove the meat and turnips from the liquid and cut into 1-inch cubes. To the meat and turnips, add chopped onions (including tops), prepared sesame seed, soy sauce, and pepper. Mix well. Cook for 2 minutes or until seasonings are absorbed. Return to the liquid and reheat. Season with salt and decorate each bowl of soup with egg.

Use 1 egg. To prepare for decoration, see page 11. When prepared, roll each piece separately into a long tube shape and shred crosswise.

MEAT DUMPLINGS

(Man-tu)

1 lb. beef	2 tsp oil
2 green onions	¼ cup mushrooms
2 tbsp. prepared sesame seed (see recipe p. 11)	1 cup bean sprouts
6 tbsp. soy sauce	1 tsp. salt
1½ cloves garlic	1 cup chopped cooked celery cabbage
speck pepper	3 tbsp. pine nuts
7 cups water	1 egg

Soup: Cut ¼ lb. beef into thin slices 1 inch square. Add 1 chopped onion (including top), 1 tbsp. prepared sesame seed, 2 tbsp. soy sauce, ½ clove chopped garlic, and pepper. Mix well. Cook until meat is well seared. Add water and cook until meat is tender.

Filling: Grind ¾ lb. beef fine and add 1 chopped onion (including top), 1 tbsp. prepared sesame seed, 4 tbsp. soy sauce, 1 clove chopped garlic, 2 tsp. oil, and pepper. Mix well. Chop mushrooms fine and add to the meat. If fresh bean sprouts are used, prepare by removing the bean and hairlike end on each sprout. Cook in boiling water 3 minutes and chop fine. Prepare canned sprouts by removing beans. Chop the sprouts finely. Add to the meat. (The beans removed from the sprouts are not used in this recipe.) Chop celery cabbage finely. Boil for 3 minutes in a small amount of water, press out liquid and add to the meat. Add salt and mix we   together.

Dough

   3 cups flour

   1 cup water

Add water to the flour to make a stiff dough. Knead 5 minutes. Roll the dough into a long piece 1 inch in diameter and cut crosswise into 1-inch lengths. Roll each piece into a circle 3 inches in diameter. Put 1 spoonful of the meat mixture on the lower half of the circle of dough Add 2 or 3 pine nuts. Fold the dough over to make a half circle. Press edges firmly together to hold the meat inside.

When ready to serve, drop dumplings into the boiling soup. When the dumplings come to the top, cook 2 minutes longer and serve at once. Serve 6–8 dumplings per person. Decorate the top of each bowl of soup and dumplings with egg.

Use 1 egg. To prepare for decoration, see recipe on page 11. Cut into 1/2-inch diamond-shaped pieces and use yolk and white as decoration for each bowl of soup.

RIBS SOUP
(Kah-ri kook)

2 lbs. ribs	2 tbsp. prepared sesame
14 cups water	seed (see recipe p. 11)
6 tbsp. soy sauce	speck pepper
4 green onions	salt
2 cloves garlic	1 egg

Cut ribs into pieces 2–3 inches long, 1–2 inches wide. Cut across each rib into the bone 3 or 4 times. Put into a pan, add cold water and cook until tender (about 1½ hours). Remove the ribs from the liquid and add to them the soy sauce, chopped onions (including tops), chopped garlic, prepared sesame seed, and pepper. Mix well. Cook together for 5 minutes, or until the seasonings are well absorbed. Remove excess fat from the liquid in which the ribs were cooked. Put ribs back into the liquid. Cook slowly for 1 hour, or until the meat is very tender. Season with salt. Decorate each bowl of soup with egg.

Use 1 egg. To prepare for decoration, see recipe on page 11. When prepared, roll separately into a long tube shape and shred crosswise very finely.

SUMMER MEAT DUMPLINGS

(*Pyun-su*)

1 small chicken	1 tbsp. soy sauce
1 onion	1 tbsp. sesame seed
1 cucumber	⅛ tsp. pepper
¼ carrot	1 egg
½ cup mushrooms	2 tbsp. pine nuts
¼ cup chopped celery	oil

Clean chicken and cut in pieces. Cover with boiling salted water and cook until tender. Remove the chicken and cut in thin flat pieces 1 inch long. Cool the chicken broth and remove all the fat. To the chicken, add soy sauce, sesame seed, and pepper. Mix well.

Chop onion fine.

Cut cucumber in fine strips. Add ¼ tsp. salt and let stand a few minutes. Drain off all liquid and fry for 1 minute in ½ tsp. oil.

Shred carrot and cook for a few minutes in boiling water.

Drain well.

Chop mushrooms and celery.

Fry together in 1 tsp. oil, the onion, carrot, mushrooms, and celery.

Put chicken and vegetables together and season with salt.

Dough

3 cups flour
1 cup water

Add water to the flour to make a stiff dough. Knead five minutes. Roll the dough very thin and cut in 3-inch squares. Place a spoonful of the chicken mixture in the center of each square. Add 3 pine nuts. Bring the four points of the square to the center above the chicken mixture and twist the points together. Press edges together tightly.

Drop dumplings in rapidly boiling water. The balls will sink to the bottom. After they rise to the top of the water, cook one more minute. Remove the balls to soup bowls and cool. Pour over them the cold chicken broth and decorate each bowl with egg. To prepare for egg decoration see page 11. When prepared, cut into ½-inch diamond-shaped pieces.

CHICKEN SOUP

(Dahk kook)

1 chicken	speck pepper
5 tbsp. soy sauce	8 cups liquid
1 green onion	1 tsp. salt
1 clove garlic	1 egg

Clean chicken and cut from the bone in 1-inch pieces. Make a broth from the bones to use as part of the liquid for the soup. Add soy sauce to the chicken, chopped onion (including top), chopped garlic, and pepper. Mix well and cook until chicken is well seared. Add broth made from the chicken bones, plus enough water to make 8 cups. Cook until chicken is tender. Season with salt. Decorate each bowl of soup with egg.

Use 1 egg. To prepare for decoration, see page 11. When prepared, roll each piece separately into a long tube shape and shred crosswise.

VEGETABLES

Vegetables fit for use are re-
cognized by the smallest sprout.

(KOREAN PROVERB)

Vegetables are used commonly in the every-day diet in Korea. In addition to those eaten by most people around the world, Korea has many interesting roots, leaves, mosses, and sprouts.

FRIED SWEET POTATOES
(Ko-koo-mah juhn)

2 medium sweet potatoes	3 tbsp. oil
3 tbsp. flour	salt
1 egg	

Wash, peel, and cut sweet potatoes crosswise into ¼-inch slices. Cook in boiling, salted water until partially done. Roll in flour, then in slightly beaten egg. Fry in a small amount of oil until light brown. Season with salt. Serve with vinegar-soy sauce (see recipe page 12).

FRIED SQUASH
(Ho-pahk juhn)

1 summer squash	2½ tbsp. oil
3 tbsp. flour	salt
1 egg	

Wash and cut the squash crosswise into ¼-inch slices. Roll in flour, then in slightly beaten egg. Fry slowly in a small amount of oil until light brown on both sides. Season with salt. Serve with vinegar-soy sauce (see recipe page 12).

FRIED EGG PLANT
(Kah-ri juhn)

1 medium egg plant	2 tbsp. oil
3 tbsp. flour	salt
1 egg	

Wash, peel, and cut egg plant into pieces 2 inches long, 1 inch wide, and ¼ inch thick. Dip in flour, then in slightly beaten egg. Fry slowly in a small amount of oil until light brown on both sides. Serve with vinegar-soy sauce (see recipe page 12).

FRIED SPINACH

(See-kum-chee juhn)

1 lb. spinach	2½ tbsp. oil
4 tbsp flour	salt
2 eggs	

Choose small tender bunches of spinach. Remove roots, leaving just enough to hold leaves together. Wash carefully. Cook in boiling water for a few minutes. Remove and press out all water. Skewer several spinach plants by root ends on a toothpick. Trim spinach so that it is not longer than 3 inches. Prepare all the spinach in this way. Dip skewered pieces in flour, then in slightly beaten egg. Fry in a small amount of oil until light brown on both sides. Season with salt. Remove toothpicks and serve with vinegar-soy sauce (see recipe page 12).

FRIED GREEN PEPPERS

(Ko-chooh juhn)

6 very small peppers	2 tbsp. soy sauce
¼ lb. beef	1 clove garlic
1 tbsp. prepared sesame seed (see recipe p. 11)	1 tbsp. flour
	1 egg
speck pepper	2½ tbsp. oil

Wash peppers. Cut into halves lengthwise, and remove seeds. Chop beef fine, add prepared sesame seed, pepper, soy sauce, and chopped garlic. Mix well. Pack the peppers level full with the meat mixture. Dip the meat-side of the pepper in flour, then roll the whole pepper in slightly beaten egg. Fry slowly in a small amount of oil until meat and pepper are tender. Serve with vinegar-soy sauce (see recipe page 12).

FRIED ONIONS

(Ok-chong juhn)

3 medium onions
4 tbsp. flour
2 eggs
4 tbsp. oil
salt

Wash onions and remove the outside skin. Cut in halves lengthwise, then cut in ¼-inch wedge-shaped pieces, being careful not to separate the layers of onion. If necessary, fasten the layers of onion together with toothpicks. Roll in flour, then in slightly beaten egg. Fry slowly in a small amount of oil until light brown. Season with salt. Serve with vinegar-soy sauce (see recipe page 12).

FRIED POTATO, ONION AND CARROT

(Cha-soh juhn)

1 medium potato
1 medium onion
1 medium carrot
2 eggs
¾ cup flour
¼ cup water
1 tsp. salt
2 tbsp. oil

Cut the vegetables in 1½-inch lengths and shred lengthwise very fine. Beat the eggs slightly with a fork. Add flour, salt, and water. Beat well. Add the vegetables and mix lightly. Drop by teaspoonfuls in oblong shape on a heated, oiled skillet. Fry slowly in a small amount of oil until light brown on both sides. Serve with vinegar-soy sauce (see recipe page 12).

FRIED WHITE POTATOES

(Kam-ja juhn)

4 small potatoes	2 tbsp. oil
3 tbsp. flour	salt
1 egg	

Wash potatoes, peel and cut crosswise into 1/4-inch slices. Cook in salted, boiling water until partially done. Roll in flour, then in slightly beaten egg. Fry in a small amount of oil until light brown. Season with salt. Serve with vinegar-soy sauce (see recipe page 12).

BLACK BEANS

(Khong ja-pahn)

1/2 cup black beans	1/2 tsp. chopped red
1 1/4 cup water	chile pepper
4 tbsp. soy sauce	1 tbsp. prepared sesame
1/2 tsp. candied ginger	seed (see recipe p. 11)
1 1/2 tbsp. sugar	1 tbsp. oil

Wash beans well. Add water and cook until partially done. Combine soy sauce, chopped ginger, sugar, chopped chile pepper, prepared sesame seed, and oil. Add to the beans. Cook slowly until the water has been absorbed. The beans will be hard and salty. They are eaten in small amounts with rice.

BEAN SPROUTS

(Khong na-mool)

4 cups bean sprouts	1 1/2 tsp. oil
2 1/2 tbsp. soy sauce	2 green onions
2 tbsp. prepared sesame	speck red pepper
seed (see recipe p. 11)	1 tsp. salt

Wash fresh bean sprouts and remove the hairlike end from each sprout (for directions for sprouting beans at home, see page 12). Cover with boiling water and cook until tender. Drain. Add soy sauce, prepared sesame seed, oil, chopped onion (reserving the tops), and red pepper. Reheat until seasonings are all absorbed. When almost done, cut onion tops in 1-inch lengths and add to bean sprouts, cooking until tender. Season with salt.

BEETS IN SOY SAUCE
(Beets na-mool)

6 large beets	1 tsp. oil
2 tbsp. soy sauce	2 tbsp. vinegar
1 tsp. prepared sesame seed (see recipe p. 11)	1 tsp. sugar
	1 tsp. salt

Wash, peel, and cook beets. When almost done add the beet tops which have been cut into 2-inch lengths. Cook until tender. Drain. Cut the beets into pieces 1 inch long, ¼ inch wide, and ¼ inch thick. Combine with the tops and add soy sauce, prepared sesame seed, oil, vinegar, sugar, and salt. Mix lightly.

SPINACH AND BEEF
(See-kum-chee na-mool)

1½ lbs. spinach	1 tbsp. prepared sesame seed (see recipe p. 11)
¼ lb. beef	
speck red pepper	2 tbsp. soy sauce
1 green onion	1 tsp. oil
1 clove garlic	1 tbsp. sugar
	salt

Remove roots and separate the leaves of the spinach. Wash until free from sand and dirt. Cook in a small amount of water only until tender. Do not overcook. Drain and press out all the water. Cut in 2-inch lengths. Chop beef fine. Add pepper, chopped onion (including top), chopped garlic, prepared sesame seed, soy sauce, oil, and sugar. Mix well. Cook until meat is well seared. Mix meat with the spinach and season with salt. Serve hot or cold.

CABBAGE-CARROT-CELERY SALAD

(Cho na-mool)

3 cups shredded celery
   cabbage
1 cup shredded carrot
¼ cup shredded celery
1½ tsp. salt
½ tsp. oil
2 tbsp. sugar
1 tbsp. vinegar

Cut celery cabbage into 1½-inch lengths. Peel carrot and cut into 1½-inch lengths. Shred celery and carrot lengthwise, very finely. Cook for 3 minutes in a small amount of boiling, salted water. Drain and cool.

Cut the celery into 1½-inch lengths. Shred lengthwise. Sprinkle with ½ tsp. salt and let stand 10 minutes. Then wash, drain, and fry in a small amount of oil for 3 minutes, stirring constantly. Cool. Mix vegetables. Add 1 tsp. salt, sugar, and vinegar. Mix lightly. Mustard may be used for seasoning, if desired.

LETTUCE

(Sang-chee na-mool)

3 medium bunches leaf
   lettuce
3 tbsp. soy sauce
1 green onion

1½ tbsp. prepared
   sesame seed
   (see recipe p. 11)
speck red pepper
½ tsp. oil

Wash the lettuce well. Mix together soy sauce, chopped onion (including top), prepared sesame seed, red pepper, and oil. Arrange a layer of lettuce leaves on a plate attractively. Add 1 tbsp. soy sauce mixture, then another layer of lettuce, then sauce until used up. This dish should resemble a large flower when it is completed.

CARROT-TURNIP-CUCUMBER SALAD

(Tang-kun na-mool)

2 carrots	1½ tsp. salt
2 turnips	4 tbsp. sugar
1 cucumber	4 tbsp. vinegar

Wash, peel, and cut carrots and turnips into 1-inch lengths. Shred lengthwise. Wash cucumber and, without peeling, cut into 2-inch lengths. Cut into halves lengthwise and remove seeds. Shred lengthwise in fine pieces. Combine vegetables. Add salt, sugar, and vinegar. Mix lightly. If desired, bamboo shoots may be added.

STRING BEANS

(Keen-Kong na-mool)

3 cups string beans
¼ lb. beef
1 tbsp. sesame seed
2 tbsp. soy sauce
1 green onion
1 tsp. sugar
1 tsp. oil

Wash beans and cut into 1½-inch lengths. Cook in a small amount of water for only a few minutes. They should be a bright green color. Drain off the water.

Chop beef fine. Add sesame seed, soy sauce, chopped green onion, sugar, and oil. Mix well. Cook until the meat is done. Add beans and cook until beans are slightly tender. Do not overcook.

VEGETABLE-PORK SALAD

(Chai-yuk sang-cha)

¼ lb. pork
1 tsp. chopped ginger
1 tsp. chopped garlic
1 tbsp. chopped green onion
1 cup turnip
salt
1 small round onion
½ cup mushrooms
oil

1 small carrot
1 cup celery or fresh spinach
1 hard pear
2 tbsp. soy sauce
2 tbsp. sugar
¼ tsp. pepper
2 tsp. vinegar
1 tsp. pine nuts

Boil pork until tender. Cut in fine strips 2 inches long. Chop ginger, garlic, and green onion. Add to the pork.

Wash and peel turnip. Cut in 2-inch strips the same as the pork. Add 1 tsp. salt and let stand 10 minutes. Drain and fry in a small amount of oil.

Cut onion in pieces the same size as the turnip. Fry in a small amount of oil.

Cut mushrooms the same size as the turnip. Fry in a small amount of oil.

Wash and peel carrot. Cut in pieces the same as the turnip. Boil for 2–3 minutes in a small amount of water. Drain.

Wash and cut celery in pieces the same as the turnip. Add 1 tsp. salt and let stand for 10 minutes. Drain well and fry in a small amount of oil for a few minutes, or until a bright green color. If spinach is used, wash well and cook only until it is tender.

Wash, peel and cut pear in the same size as the turnip.

Combine pork, vegetables, and pear. Combine soy sauce, sugar, pepper, and vinegar. Mix lightly with the pork and vegetable mixture. Arrange on a plate and sprinkle the top with chopped pine nuts.

CARROT-TURNIP SALAD

(Moo sang-cha)

2 turnips
2 carrots
1 tsp. salt
2 tbsp. vinegar
1 tbsp. sugar
speck red pepper

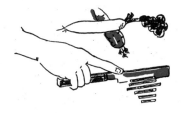

Wash and peel turnips and carrots. Cut into 2-inch lengths. Shred lengthwise. Add salt, vinegar, sugar, and pepper. Mix lightly.

TURNIP-BEEF SALAD

(Moo sang-cha)

2 cups shredded turnip
1 tbsp. soy sauce
1 tsp. salt
speck red pepper
¼ cup chopped beef
1 tsp. chopped green onion
½ tsp. chopped garlic

1 tsp. prepared sesame seed (see recipe p. 11)
⅛ tsp. pepper
1 tsp oil
½ tsp. vinegar
2 tsp. sugar
2 tsp. pine nuts

Wash, peel, and shred turnips. Sprinkle with salt and let stand 10 minutes. Drain off any water that forms. Add 2 tsp. soy sauce and red pepper. Mix well.

Chop beef fine. Add chopped onion, chopped garlic, 1 tsp. soy sauce, sesame seed, pepper and oil. Mix well. Cook until the meat is done. Combine meat and turnip. Add vinegar and sugar. Mix together lightly. Arrange on a small plate and sprinkle the top with chopped pine nuts.

CUCUMBERS WITH BEEF

(O-i jim)

6 medium cucumbers
2 tbsp. salt
3 tbsp. oil
¼ lb. beef
1 tbsp. soy sauce
1 tbsp. prepared sesame
    seed (see recipe p. 11)
speck black pepper
1 clove garlic
2 red chile peppers
1 tbsp. pine nuts
1 egg

Wash cucumber and trim off the stem end. Cut 3 slits lengthwise at equal distances around the cucumber, being careful not to break it. Sprinkle with salt and let stand 15 minutes. Wash off the salt and squeeze out the water. Heat the oil in a skillet and fry the cucumbers until they are bright green, turning often. Do not overcook.

Chop the beef fine. Add soy sauce, prepared sesame seed, pepper, and chopped garlic. Mix well. Pack this mixture into the slits of the cucumber. Shred the chile peppers very fine and insert a little in each slit. Put pine nuts at equal distances in the slits.

Use 1 egg. To prepare for decoration, see page 11. When prepared, roll each layer into a long tube and shred crosswise very fine. Insert shreds of egg into the slits of the cucumber.

Fry the cucumbers again slowly, turning often, until the meat is done. Arrange on a plate and decorate with remaining shredded egg.

SQUASH WITH BEEF

(Ho-pahk jim)

2 summer squash
¼ lb. beef
speck pepper
3 tbsp. soy sauce
1 tbsp. prepared sesame
    seed (see recipe p. 11)
1 green onion
1 clove garlic
1 tbsp. oil
1 red chile pepper
2 eggs
salt
1½ cups water

Cut each squash crosswise in 2-inch lengths. With cut side up, score each piece ¾ of the way down to form pattern of ¼-inch squares.

Chop beef fine. Add pepper, 1 tbsp. soy sauce, prepared sesame seed, chopped onion (including top), chopped garlic, and oil. Mix well. Pack half the meat mixture into the slits of the squash, being careful not to break the squash. Shred the chile pepper into very fine pieces and insert a little in each slit.

Use 2 eggs. To prepare for decoration, see page 11. When prepared, roll each piece into a long tube shape and shred crosswise. Insert bits of the egg into the slits of the squash.

Put the meat that remains in the bottom of a pan. Add squash and sprinkle remaining egg over the top. Add water to ⅓ the depth of the squash, and 2 tbsp. soy sauce. Cover and cook slowly until tender. Season with salt.

MEAT AND VEGETABLES WITH VERMICELLI

(Chop-chai)

½ cup chopped beef	1 tsp. salt
2½ tbsp. soy sauce	1 cup bean sprouts or
2 green onions	celery cabbage
1 clove garlic, chopped	¼ cup mushrooms
1 tbsp. prepared sesame	1 cup vermicelli
seed (see recipe p. 11)	1 tbsp. sugar
speck pepper	1 egg
2 tsp. oil	1 firm pear
½ cup cooked pork	2 tbsp. pine nuts
½ cup celery	

Chop beef fine and add 1 tbsp. soy sauce, 1 chopped onion (including top), the chopped garlic, ½ tbsp. prepared sesame seed, pepper, and ½ tsp. oil. Cook until the meat is tender.

Wash celery and cut into 1½-inch lengths. Shred lengthwise. Add 1 tsp. salt and let stand 10 minutes. Wash, drain, and fry slowly in ½ tsp. oil for 2 minutes stirring constantly.

Cut cooked pork into 1-inch lengths and shred.

Prepare fresh bean sprouts by removing skins from the beans and the fine hairlike end from each sprout. Cook for 3 minutes in boiling water and drain well. If canned bean sprouts are used, drain but do not cook them. If using celery cabbage instead of bean sprouts, shred and cook 3 minutes in a small amount of boiling water. Drain well, and press out all water.

Shred mushrooms and fry in ½ tsp. oil. Season with salt.

Cook vermicelli in rapidly boiling water for 6 minutes. Drain well and cut into 3-inch lengths.

Use 1 egg. To prepare for decoration, see recipe on

p. 11. When prepared, roll each layer separately into a long tube shape and shred crosswise.

Wash, peel and shred pear into fine strips an inch long.

To combine: add pork to the beef, then celery, bean sprouts, mushrooms, and remaining seasonings (1½ tbsp. soy sauce, 1 chopped onion with top, ½ tbsp. prepared sesame seed, 1 tbsp. sugar). Mix well. Lastly, add the vermicelli and shredded pear. Season with salt. Arrange on two medium sized plates and decorate with shredded egg and pine nuts.

MUSHROOMS WITH BEEF

(Song-i jim)

¼ lb. beef	1 tbsp. prepared sesame
3 tbsp. soy sauce	seed (see recipe p. 11)
1 green onion	1 cup sliced mushrooms
1 clove garlic	2 tbsp. flour
speck red pepper	2 eggs
speck black pepper	2 tbsp. oil
	½ cup water

Chop the beef fine and add 2 tbsp. soy sauce, chopped onion (reserving the top), chopped garlic, red pepper, black pepper, and prepared sesame seed. Mix well. Put a layer of beef the same thickness as a slice of mushroom between two slices of mushroom. Press together. Prepare all the mushrooms in this way. Roll in flour, then in slightly beaten egg. Fry slowly until brown on both sides.

Put any meat that is left in a pan. Add the browned mushrooms, onion tops (now cut in 2-inch lengths), water, and cook until tender and water is all absorbed. Cook the egg that remains in a thin layer in a heated, oiled skillet. When firm, turn and cook slightly on the other side. Roll into a long tube shape and shred crosswise very fine. Arrange mushrooms on a plate and decorate with the egg.

TURNIPS WITH BEEF

(Moo-sook-jang-ah-gee)

4 turnips	2 green onions
2 tbsp. salt	2 tbsp. soy sauce
¼ lb. beef	1 tsp. oil
¼ tsp. red chile pepper	speck black pepper
1 clove garlic	3 tbsp. water
2 tbsp. prepared sesame	1 tsp. candied ginger
seed (see recipe p. 11)	2 tbsp. sugar

Wash, peel, and cut turnips into 1-inch cubes. Sprinkle with salt and let stand 10 minutes. Chop beef fine. Add chopped chile pepper, chopped garlic, onions (including tops), prepared sesame seed, soy sauce, oil, and pepper. Mix well. Cook until the meat is well seared.

Wash the salt from the turnips and add them to the meat. Add water, chopped ginger, sugar, and salt, if necessary. Cook until turnips are tender.

MEAT & FOWL

The spring pheasant calls out his where-abouts. (KOREAN PROVERB)

Delicious dishes are made from beef, pork and chicken in Korea. A favorite dish is broiled beef or *pul ko-kee* which is beef seasoned and broiled over a charcoal fire.

BROILED BEEF

(Pul ko-kee)

1 lb. beef	1 green onion
4 tbsp. sugar	1 clove garlic
2 tbsp. oil	4 tbsp. prepared sesame
6 tbsp. soy sauce	seed (see recipe p. 11)
speck pepper	1 tbsp. flour
	water

Cut the beef into thin slices 3 inches square. Add sugar and oil. Mix well. Combine soy sauce, pepper, chopped onion (including top), chopped garlic, prepared sesame seed and flour. Add to the meat. Mix well.

Let stand 15 minutes. Broil on a charcoal fire, or fry in a small amount of oil until tender. If frying meat, cover tightly after it is well browned. Add a small amount of water and steam until meat is tender. Serve hot.

BROILED PORK

(Ton-yuk kui)

1 lb. pork	1 tsp. candied ginger
6 tbsp. soy sauce	2 tbsp. prepared sesame
2 tbsp. sugar	seed (see recipe p. 11)
1 green onion	1 tsp. oil
1 clove garlic	speck pepper

Cut the pork into very thin slices 3 inches square. Combine soy sauce, sugar, chopped onion (including top), chopped garlic, chopped ginger, prepared sesame seed, and pepper. Add all to the pork, mixing well.

Let stand 15 minutes. Broil or fry in a small amount of oil. If frying the pork, cover tightly after it is well browned. Add a small amount of water and steam until the pork is tender. Serve hot.

BROILED RIBS

(Kah-ri kui)

2 lbs. short ribs	1 clove garlic
3 tbsp. sugar	speck pepper
2 tbsp. oil	2 tbsp. prepared sesame
6 tbsp. soy sauce	seed (see recipe p. 11)
1 green onion	1 tbsp. flour

Have slab of ribs cut into serving pieces of about 3–4-inch squares. On both sides of each piece, score deeply every ½ inch. Add sugar and oil to the ribs. Mix well and let stand while preparing the remaining seasonings. Combine soy sauce, chopped onion (including top), chopped garlic, pepper, prepared sesame seed, and flour. Mix well with the ribs. Let stand 15–30 minutes. Broil, using medium heat and serve at once. A charcoal fire can be prepared and placed conveniently near the table to broil the ribs further, if the center is not well done. These are eaten with the fingers.

BROILED TONGUE

(Oo-sul kui)

1 lb tongue	1 green onion
2 tbsp. soy sauce	1 clove garlic
1 tbsp. prepared sesame	1 tbsp. sugar
seed (see recipe p. 11)	1 tsp. oil
speck pepper	

Remove skin and roots from the tongue and cut into thin slices 2–3 inches square. Combine soy sauce, prepared sesame seed, pepper, chopped onion (including top), chopped garlic, sugar and oil. Mix well with the tongue. Let stand 15 minutes. Broil or fry in a small amount of oil. If frying the tongue, cover tightly after it is well browned. Add a small amount of water and steam until tender.

BROILED HEART

(Yum-tong kui)

1 lb. heart	1 green onion
2 tbsp. soy sauce	1 clove garlic
1 tbsp. prepared sesame seed (see recipe p. 11)	1 tbsp. sugar
	1 tsp. oil
speck pepper	1 tbsp. flour

Clean and cut heart into thin slices 3 inches square. Combine soy sauce, prepared sesame seed, pepper, chopped onion (including top), chopped garlic, sugar, oil and flour. Mix well with the heart. Let stand 15 minutes. Broil or fry in a small amount of oil. If frying the heart, after it is well browned, cover tightly, add a small amount of water, and steam until well done.

BROILED CHICKEN

(Tak kui)

1 small chicken	1 green onion
4 tbsp. soy sauce	1 clove garlic
2 tbsp. prepared sesame seed (see recipe p. 11)	1 tbsp. sugar
	1 tsp. oil
speck pepper	

Clean the chicken and cut meat from the bones in flat slices 2-3 inches square. Combine soy sauce, prepared sesame seed, pepper, chopped onion (including top), chopped garlic, sugar, and oil. Add to the chicken. Mix well and let stand 15 minutes. Broil or fry slowly in a small amount of oil. If frying the chicken, after it is well browned, cover tightly, add a small amount of water and steam until very tender.

BROILED PHEASANT

(Gooung kui)

1 pheasant
4 tbsp. soy sauce
2 tbsp. prepared sesame
   seed (see recipe p. 11)
speck pepper
1 green onion
1 clove garlic
1 tbsp. sugar
1 tsp. oil

Clean pheasant and cut in thin, flat slices 2-3 inches square. Combine soy sauce, prepared sesame seed, pepper, chopped onion (including top), chopped garlic, sugar and oil. Add to the pheasant. Mix well and let stand for 11 minutes. Broil or fry in a small amount of oil until tender.

BEEF AND ONIONS ON SKEWERS

(Pah sahn-juhk)

½ lb. beef
1 bunch tender green
   onions
2 tbsp. soy sauce
2 tbsp. prepared sesame
   seed (see recipe p. 11)

speck pepper
1 clove garlic
1 tbsp. sugar
2½ tbsp. oil
3 tbsp. flour
1 egg

Cut the beef into strips 2 inches long, ¼ inch wide, ¼ inch thick. Count the number of pieces of beef and cut the same number of pieces of onion slightly longer than the meat. Combine soy sauce, prepared sesame seed, pepper, chopped garlic, sugar, and 1 tsp. oil. Add to the beef. Let stand 15 minutes. Run the skewer through a piece of meat, then a piece of onion, then meat and onion until there are six pieces on the skewer. Prepare all the meat and onions in this way. Dip each piece in flour, then in slightly beaten egg. Fry slowly on both sides until meat and onions are tender.

BEEF ON SKEWERS

(Oo-yuk sahn-juhk)

½ lb. lean beef
2 tbsp. soy sauce
2 tbsp. prepared sesame
  seed (see recipe p. 11)
speck pepper
1 green onion
1 clove garlic
1 tbsp. sugar
2 tbsp. oil

Cut beef into strips 3 inches long, ¼ inch wide and ¼ inch thick. Combine soy sauce, 1 tbsp. prepared sesame seed, pepper, chopped onion (including top), chopped garlic, sugar, ½ tbsp. oil. Mix with the meat. Let stand 15 minutes. Run a skewer through the ends of 5 or 6 pieces of beef. Press together and pound slightly to make the pieces adhere to each other. Sprinkle with remaining sesame seed and fry in a small amount of oil. Carefully remove the skewers before serving.

BEEF AND MUSHROOMS ON SKEWERS

(Song-i sahn-juhk)

¼ lb. beef	1 green onion
6 large mushrooms	1 clove garlic
1 tbsp. soy sauce	½ tbsp. sugar
1 tbsp. prepared sesame seed (see recipe p. 11)	1 tbsp. oil
	3 tbsp. flour
speck pepper	1 egg

Cut the mushrooms lengthwise into 4-6 pieces. Cut the beef into pieces the same length as the mushrooms, ¼ inch wide and ¼ inch thick. Combine soy sauce, prepared sesame seed, pepper, chopped onion (including top), chopped garlic, sugar, and oil. Add to the meat and mushrooms. Let stand 15 minutes. Put a skewer through the end of a piece of mushroom, then meat, then mushroom, until there are 6 pieces on the skewer. Prepare all the meat and mushrooms in this way. Press the strips on each skewer together, roll in flour, then in slightly beaten egg. Fry in a small amount of oil until brown on both sides and well done.

PHEASANT "POK-KUM"

(Gooung pok-kum)

1 pheasant	speck pepper
6 tbsp. soy sauce	1 tsp. oil
2 green onions	2 tbsp. sugar
2 cloves garlic	½ cup sliced mushrooms
3 tbsp. prepared sesame seed (see recipe p. 11)	salt

Clean and bone the pheasant and cut into pieces 1 inch square. Cover with boiling water and cook slowly until partially done. Remove the pheasant from the liquid and add to the pheasant the soy sauce, chopped onions (including tops), chopped garlic, prepared sesame seed, pepper, oil, sugar, and sliced mushrooms. Mix well. Add enough liquid in which pheasant was cooked to cover pheasant partially, and continue cooking until very tender.

HEART "POK-KUM"
(Yum-tong pok-kum)

½ lb. heart	speck pepper
1 large onion	1 tsp. oil
2 tbsp. soy sauce	2 tbsp. sugar
1 clove garlic	½ cup water
1 tbsp. prepared sesame seed (see recipe p. 11)	salt

Cut the heart into very thin slices 1½ inch long and 1 inch wide. Combine soy sauce, chopped garlic, prepared sesame seed, pepper, oil, and sugar. Add to the heart. Clean and cut onion into quarters then slice each quarter in 4 pieces crosswise. Add to the heart and cook 5 minutes. Add water and cook until tender. Season with salt.

LIVER "POK-KUM"
(Kan pok-kum)

½ lb. liver	1 tsp. oil
2 tbsp. soy sauce	1½ tbsp. sugar
1 clove garlic	1 large onion
speck pepper	½ cup water
1 tbsp. prepared sesame seed (see recipe p. 11)	salt

Cut the liver into very thin slices 1½ inches long and 1 inch wide. Combine soy sauce, chopped garlic, pepper, prepared sesame seed, oil, and sugar. Add to the liver. Clean and cut onion in quarters and each quarter into 4 slices crosswise. Add to the liver. Cook 5 minutes. Add water and cook until tender. Season with salt.

CHICKEN "POK-KUM"

(Tahk pok-kum)

1 small chicken	3 tbsp prepared sesame
6 tbsp. soy sauce	seed (see recipe p. 11)
2 green onions	2 tbsp. sugar
2 cloves garlic	½ cup sliced mushrooms
speck pepper	salt

Clean the chicken. Using a heavy knife, cut through the meat and bone into pieces 1 inch square. Cover with boiling water and cook slowly until partially done. Combine soy sauce, chopped onions (including tops), chopped garlic, pepper, prepared sesame seed, and sugar. Mix well. Remove the chicken from the liquid and add it to the combined seasonings. Add sliced mushrooms. Add enough of the liquid in which the chicken was cooked to half cover the chicken and mushrooms and continue cooking until chicken is very tender. Season with salt.

BEEF "POK-KUM"

(Song-i pok-kum)

¼ lb. beef	1 tbsp. prepared sesame
6 large mushrooms	seed (see recipe p. 11)
2 tbsp. soy sauce	1 tsp. oil
1 green onion	½ tsp. candied ginger
1 clove garlic	salt
speck pepper	¼ cup water
	1 egg

Grind the beef fine. Slice mushrooms 1½ inch long and ¼ inch wide. Combine soy sauce, chopped onion (including top), chopped garlic, pepper, prepared sesame seed, oil, and chopped ginger. Add to the meat. Mix in the mushrooms and cook all together 5 minutes. Season with salt. Add water and continue cooking until tender. If desired, stir a slightly beaten egg into the mixture just before serving, or use the egg as decoration.

Use 1 egg. To prepare for decoration, see recipe on page 11. When prepared roll each layer into a long tube shape and shred crosswise. Sprinkle over the top of the meat and mushrooms.

SALTED BEEF SQUARES

(Jang-san juhk)

½ lb. beef
¾ cup soy sauce
1 green onion
1 clove garlic
speck pepper
2 tbsp. prepared sesame
  seed (see recipe p. 11)
1 tbsp. oil
¼ cup water
3 tbsp. sugar
1 tbsp. pine nuts

Chop the beef fine. Combine 3 tbsp. soy sauce, chopped onion (including top), chopped garlic, pepper, and 1 tbsp. prepared sesame seed. Mix well with the beef. Shape the beef into 4 flat squares ½ inch thick. Press each until firm. Sprinkle with 1 tbsp. prepared sesame seed. Fry the squares slowly until done in the center. Cut into 1 inch squares. Put the squares of meat in a pan. Add remaining soy sauce, water, and sugar. Cook until the beef is dark brown. Remove from the liquid. Arrange attractively on a plate and sprinkle the top with chopped pine nuts. This is a very salty dish and is eaten in small amounts with rice.

DRIED BEEF

(Yuk-poh)

1 lb. beef
5 tbsp. soy sauce
1 tsp. salt
3 tbsp. sugar
2 tbsp. oil
¼ tsp. pepper
3 tbsp. pine nuts

Cut beef into slices ¼ inch thick. Combine soy sauce, salt, sugar, oil, and pepper. Add to the beef. Mix well. Spread the slices of beef on a wire rack. Sprinkle with finely chopped pine nuts and place in the sun for two days or until thoroughly dried. Place where the air circulates freely. When well dried, broil and cut into 1-inch squares for serving.

SALTED BEEF

(Jahng jo-rim)

¼ lb. beef
2 cups boiling water
1/3 cup soy sauce
3 tbsp. sugar
1 tsp. candied ginger

Add water to the beef and cook until tender. Add soy sauce, sugar, and chopped ginger. Continue cooking until the beef is dark brown and only a small amount of liquid remains. Tear into strips 1½ inch long and ¼ inch wide. This meat is very salty and is eaten in small amounts with rice.

BOILED RIBS WITH VEGETABLES

(Kah-ri-jim)

2 lbs. ribs	speck pepper
2 tbsp. sugar	2 tbsp. flour
2 tbsp. oil	1 carrot
½ cup soy sauce	6 mushrooms
3 green onions	1½ cups water
2 cloves garlic	2 tbsp. pine nuts
3 tbsp. prepared sesame seed (see recipe p. 11)	1 egg

Have slab of ribs cut into serving pieces of about 3–4 inches square. On both sides of each piece, score deeply every ½ inch. Add sugar and oil. Mix well. Combine soy sauce, chopped onions (including tops), chopped garlic, prepared sesame seed, pepper, and flour. Mix with the ribs. Wash, peel and cut carrots in pieces 1 inch long, ¼ inch wide, ¼ inch thick. Add to the meat. Slice mushrooms. Add to the meat. Add just enough water to cover the ribs and cook until tender. Arrange on a plate and decorate the top with pine nuts and shredded egg.

To prepare for egg decoration, see page 11. Then roll each layer into a long tube shape and shred crosswise.

BOILED TONGUE

(Oo-suhl puen-yuk)

1 lb. tongue	2 tbsp. soy sauce
2 cups water	1 tsp. salt

Wash the tongue. Add boiling water and cook until tender. When almost tender, remove the skin of the tongue add soy sauce, salt, and cook 15 minutes longer. Cool thoroughly and cut as thin as possible into slices 2 inches long and 1 inch wide. Serve with vinegar-soy sauce (see recipe page 12).

BOILED BEEF AND BOILED PORK
(Oo-yuk puen-yuk)

1 lb. beef or pork
2 cups water
2 tbsp. soy sauce
1 tsp. salt

Add boiling water and salt to the meat and cook until tender. When almost done, add the soy sauce and cook 15 minutes longer. Remove from the liquid and cool thoroughly. Cut as thin as possible into slices 2 inches long and 1 inch wide. Arrange attractively on a small plate and serve with vinegar-soy sauce (see recipe page 12).

BEEF AND VEGETABLES COOKED AT THE TABLE
(Juhn-kol)

3 onions
3 cups celery
3 cups celery cabbage
½ cup sliced mushrooms
2 carrots
6 eggs
½ lb. beef
¼ cup sugar
½ cup soy sauce

2 tbsp. prepared sesame seed (see recipe p. 11)
speck pepper
1 green onion
1 clove garlic
2 tbsp. oil
2 tbsp. pine nuts
beef broth or water

Clean and cut the onions into halves lengthwise and slice in ⅛ inch slices.

Wash and cut celery into strips 1½ inches long and ¼ inch wide.

Wash and cut celery cabbage into small pieces.

Clean and slice mushrooms into thin slices.

Wash, peel and cut carrots into 2-inch lengths and shred lengthwise.

Arrange the prepared vegetables attractively on a large plate using celery leaves for decoration. Sprinkle the mushrooms over the top. In the center of the vegetables place 1 uncooked, unbroken egg, point down.

Cut beef in very thin slices 2 inches square. Add sugar, 4 tbsp. soy sauce, prepared sesame seed, pepper, chopped onion (including top), chopped garlic, and oil. Mix well. Arrange on a small plate and sprinkle the top with finely chopped pine nuts.

This dish is to be cooked at the table over a charcoal burner or an electric plate. Cook the meat until well seared. Then add the vegetables and enough water or beef broth to keep it from burning. Add the remaining soy sauce and cook until meat and vegetables are tender. Steam an egg for each person by pushing aside the meat and vegetables making room for the egg to be dropped into the broth. Cover, and steam until done. Serve with rice.

FRIED BEEF BALLS

(Wan-jah juhn)

½ lb. beef	1 tbsp. prepared sesame
3 tbsp. soy sauce	seed (see recipe p. 11)
¼ tsp. salt	3 tbsp. oil
1 green onion	speck pepper
1 clove garlic	3 tbsp. flour
	2 eggs

Chop the beef fine. Add soy sauce, salt, chopped onion (including top), chopped garlic, prepared sesame seed, oil, and pepper. Mix well. Shape into flattened balls 1½ inches in diameter. Roll in flour and slightly beaten egg. Fry in a small amount of oil until tender. Serve with vinegar-soy sauce (see recipe page 12).

FRIED LIVER

(Kahn juhn)

½ lb. liver	1 egg
1 tsp. salt	2 tbsp. oil
2 tbsp. flour	

Place liver in boiling water and cook 3 minutes. Drain. Remove all skin and slice liver into thin slices about ⅛ inch thick. Sprinkle with salt, roll in flour and in slightly beaten egg. Fry in a small amount of oil. Cut in pieces 2 inches long and 1 inch wide. Arrange attractively on a plate and serve with vinegar-soy sauce (see recipe on page 12).

CHICKEN WITH VEGETABLES

(Tahk jim)

1 small chicken	1 tbsp. sesame seed
1 onion	¼ tsp. salt
1 carrot	1 tbsp. sugar
¼ cup mushrooms	speck pepper
2 bamboo shoots	2 tbsp. soy sauce
1/3 cup chestnuts	1 egg
¼ cup walnuts	3 tbsp. pine nuts

Clean chicken and cut in pieces. Cut the breast into several small pieces.

Cut onion, carrot, mushrooms and bamboo shoots into thin, flat pieces about 1 inch long. Peel the chestnuts and shell the walnuts. Mix chicken, vegetables, and nuts together. Add sesame seed, salt, sugar, pepper, and soy sauce. Add enough water to just cover the mixture. Cook until chicken is tender, and water is all absorbed. Serve in a bowl. Decorate the top with egg and pine nuts.

To prepare for egg decoration, see page 11. When prepared, cut into diamond-shaped pieces about 1 inch long.

SIN-SUL-LO

The *sin-sul-lo* is similar to a chafing dish in that food is cooked in it at the table. It is a metal bowl with a small stem in the center which holds burning charcoal. This recipe is for a *sin-sul-lo* of about 6–7 inches in diameter. To fit it, ingredients should be cut in 2-inch lengths.

½ lb. beef
3 tsp. sugar
6 tbsp. soy sauce
2 cloves garlic
speck pepper
2 tbsp prepared sesame seed (see recipe p. 11)
4 tbsp oil
⅛ lb. liver
salt
4 tbsp. flour
3 eggs
¼ lb. small tender spinach
3 mushrooms
2 tbsp. pine nuts
9 pistachio nuts
2 walnuts
3 turnips

Cut a slice of beef 3 by 5 inches in size and weighing about ⅛ lb. Combine 1 tsp. sugar, 1 tbsp. soy sauce, ½ clove chopped garlic, pepper, 2 tsp. prepared sesame seed, and 1 tsp. oil. Add to the meat. Let stand 15 minutes. Fry in a small amount of oil until tender. Cut into pieces 1 inch wide and as long as the radius of the *sin-sul-lo*.

Chop ⅛ lb. beef very fine. Add 2 tbsp. soy sauce, 1 tbsp. prepared sesame seed, ½ clove chopped garlic, 1 tsp. oil, and pepper. Mix well. Roll the mixture into tiny balls ¼ inch in diameter enclosing 1 pine nut in the center of each ball. Roll in flour, then in slightly beaten egg. Fry in a small amount of oil until done.

Cut ¼ lb. beef in thin strips 2 inches long and ½ inch wide. Add 3 tbsp. soy sauce, 2 tsp. sugar, 1 tsp. prepared sesame seed, pepper, 1 clove chopped garlic, and ½ tbsp. oil. Mix well.

Put liver in boiling water and boil 3 minutes. Remove any skin and cut into thin pieces ½ inch wide and of the same length as the *sin-sul-lo* measured from center to outside edge. Sprinkle with salt, roll in flour, then in slightly beaten egg. Fry in a small amount of oil until tender.

Remove roots and carefully wash the spinach, being careful not to separate the leaves. Put the bunches of spinach into boiling water and boil 3 minutes. Remove. Drain and press out all water. Run a skewer through the root ends of the spinach, placing 6 bunches on each skewer. Press bunches of spinach together, sprinkle with salt, roll in flour, then in slightly beaten egg. Fry in a small amount of oil. Cut into pieces ½ inch wide with the length of the radius of the *sin-sul-lo*.

Slice mushrooms the same length as the distance from the center to the outer edge of the *sin-sul-lo*. Fry slightly in a small amount of oil.

Separate the yolk and white of 1 egg. Add a speck of salt and ¼ tsp. of flour to each and beat slightly with a fork. Cook separately by circling small amounts of each over the bottom of a heated, oiled skillet. When firm, turn and cook slightly on other side. Cut egg in pieces ½ inch wide and the same length as the pieces of liver.

Prepare 1 hard-boiled egg by covering it with boiling water and letting it stand 40 minutes in a warm place. Remove the shell and cut off the ends of the egg. Cut the center into three slices to be used for decoration.

Shell and blanch the pistachio nuts. Shell and remove

the skin from the pine nuts. Carefully shell the walnuts so that the halves are not broken and blanch.

Wash, peel and boil the turnips whole in 1½ cups of boiling salted water. When done, pour off the water and save it. Cut the turnips in pieces 1½ inches long, ¼ inch wide, ¼ inch thick.

After all the food is prepared, it is arranged in the *sin-sul-lo*. In the bottom of the *sin-sul-lo,* place a layer of turnips, then a layer of uncooked beef, spinach, pieces of cooked egg, mushrooms, liver, cooked beef, until the *sin-sul-lo* is filled. Place the tiny meat balls around the center stem of the *sin-sul-lo*. Decorate with the 3 slices of hard-cooked egg, walnuts, pine nuts, and pistachio nuts. Add the water in which the turnips were cooked. Place the lid on the *sin-sul-lo* and fill the center with burning charcoal. Place on the table when ready to serve.

EGG FOLDS

(Als-sam)

¼ lb. beef	2 tbsp. soy sauce
1 green onion	4-5 eggs
1 clove garlic	½ tsp. salt
1 tbsp. prepared sesame seed (see recipe p. 11)	3 tbsp. oil

Chop the beef fine. Combine chopped onion (including top), chopped garlic, prepared sesame seed, soy sauce, and 1 tbsp. oil. Add to the meat. Mix well. Shape the beef into small pats ½ inch long, ¼ inch wide, ⅛ inch thick. Fry in a small amount of oil.

Add salt to the eggs and beat slightly with a fork. Cook the egg in thin pieces 3 inches long and 1½ inches wide. Place 1 meat ball on the lower half of the strip of cooked egg. Fold in half and press edges together. Prepare all the egg and meat this way. Serve egg folds with vinegar-soy sauce (see recipe page 12).

VEGETABLE-MEAT ROLL-UPS

(Ku chul paan)

¼ lb. beef	1 cucumber
1 tbsp. green onion	15 mushrooms
¾ tsp. chopped garlic	1 carrot
3½ tsp. sesame seed	1 cup cooked spinach
1 tsp. sugar	1 cup bean sprouts
2 tbsp. oil	3 tbsp. soy sauce
1¾ tsp. salt	1 cup flour
3 eggs	1 cup water

Chop beef fine. Add 1 tsp. chopped green onion, ¼ tsp. chopped garlic, ½ tsp. prepared sesame seed, ½ tsp. sugar, ½ tsp. oil, 1 tbsp. soy sauce, and ½ tsp. salt. Mix well. Fry in a skillet until meat is done.

Separate egg yolks and whites. Fry each separately in thin layers in a heated, oiled skillet. Shred in fine strips 2 inches long.

Cut cucumber in thin circles. Sprinkle with 1 tsp. salt and let stand 10 minutes. Press out all water that forms and fry 2 minutes in 1 tsp. oil. Season with 1½ tsp. seasame seed, ½ tsp. chopped onion, and ⅛ tsp. chopped garlic. Mix well.

Cut mushrooms in fine strips. Mix ½ tsp. sugar, ½ tsp. sesame seed, 1 tsp. soy sauce, 1 tsp. oil, and add to mushrooms. Mix well and brown in a skillet for 2 minutes.

Cut carrot in fine strips 2 inches long. Cook in boiling water for 2 minutes. Drain and add ½ tsp. chopped onion, ⅛ tsp. chopped garlic, ½ tsp. sesame seed, ¼ tsp. oil, and 2 tsp. soy sauce. Mix well.

If fresh bean sprouts are used, prepare and cook in boiling water until tender. Drain well. Mix ½ tsp. chopped onion, ⅛ tsp. chopped garlic, ½ tsp. sesame seed, ¼ tsp. oil, and 2 tsp. soy sauce. Mix well. Add to the bean sprouts. Canned bean sprouts need not be cooked.

Wash spinach and cook until just tender. Do not overcook. Press out all water that forms. Season with ½ tsp. chopped onion, ⅛ tsp. chopped garlic, ½ tsp. sesame seed, ¼ tsp. oil, and 2 tsp. soy sauce.

Mix flour and water together. Add ¼ tsp. salt. Fry in a heated oiled skillet in paper thin circles 4 inches in diameter.

Arrange attractively on a plate. Place the flat cakes in the center and the 8 foods around the cakes. In serving, put a very small portion of each food on each cake and roll it up.

SEA FOOD

Pull the fingers off a boiled crab before you eat it.

(KOREAN PROVERB)

Fish and shell fish are used widely in the Korean diet. An abundance of fresh fish and dried fish are found in the market places.

SALTED FISH

(San-suhn jo-rim)

1 lb. mackerel or perch	¼ tsp. pepper
¼ cup soy sauce	1 green onion
3 tbsp. water	1 clove garlic
1 tbsp. sugar	½ tsp. candied ginger

Skin, bone, and clean fish. Cut in pieces 1 inch square and ¼ inch thick. Add soy sauce, water, sugar, and pepper. Cut onion (including top), garlic, and ginger diagonally into thin pieces and add to the fish. Mix well and cook until the fish is tender. This is salty and is eaten in small amounts with rice.

FRIED SHRIMP

(Sao-o juhn)

2 cups cleaned shrimp	1 tsp. salt
½ cup flour	4 tbsp. oil
2 eggs	

Boil fresh shrimp 20 minutes. Remove shells and black line (the intestine) from the outside of each shrimp. Roll in flour and in slightly beaten egg. Fry in a small amount of oil until tender. Season with salt. Serve with vinegar-soy sauce (see recipe page 12). Canned shrimp is prepared in the same way, except that boiling is not necessary.

FRIED OYSTERS

(Kool juhn

2 cups oysters	4 tbsp. oil
½ cup flour	1 tsp. salt
2 eggs	

Look over the oysters and remove shells. Roll each oyster in flour, then in slightly beaten egg. Fry in a small amount of oil. Season with salt. Serve with vinegar-soy sauce (see recipe page 12).

BOILED FISH WITH VEGETABLES

(San-suhn jim)

1 white fish (2 lbs.) or	½ cup sliced mushrooms
1 lb. boned fish	½ cup bamboo sprouts
¼ lb. beef	1 carrot
1 tbsp. sugar	1 cup shredded celery
4 tbsp. soy sauce	1 cup green onion tops
1 green onion	1 tsp. chopped chile
1 clove garlic	pepper
1 tbsp. prepared sesame	1 tsp. candied ginger
seed (see recipe p. 11)	salt
speck pepper	1 egg
3 tbsp. oil	

Clean and cut the fish in half lengthwise. Remove bones and cut in flat pieces 2-3 inches square.

Chop beef fine. Add sugar, 2 tbsp. soy sauce, chopped onion (including top), chopped garlic, prepared sesame seed, pepper, and oil. Mix well.

Slice mushrooms and bamboo sprouts.

Wash, peel and cut carrots into pieces 1 inch long, ¼ inch wide, ¼ inch thick.

Wash, peel and cut celery into 2-inch lengths and shred lengthwise.

Place a layer of beef in a pan. Add a layer of bamboo sprouts, then celery, mushrooms, carrots, and fish.

Cut onion tops in 2-inch lengths and sprinkle a layer over the fish. Add bits of chopped red chile pepper and small pieces of chopped candied ginger.

Repeat until all food is used. Add water to the depth of half the fish mixture. Add remaining 2 tbsp. soy sauce and cook slowly until well done. Only a small amount of water should remain. Season with salt.

Arrange in a bowl and decorate the top with egg. Use 1 egg. To prepare for decoration, see recipe on page 11.

When prepared, roll each layer into a long tube shape and shred crosswise very fine.

FRIED LOBSTER
(Ke juhn)

2 cups lobster meat
½ cup flour
2 eggs
4 tbsp. oil
1 tsp. salt

Boil lobster 20 minutes in salted water. Cool and remove meat. Cut meat into fine pieces and firmly pack a small amount at a time into a teaspoon to form lobster meat balls. Carefully roll each ball in flour, then in slightly beaten egg.

Fry in a small amount of oil. Season with salt. Serve with vinegar-soy sauce (see recipe page 12).

FRIED FISH
(Sang-suhn juhn)

1 lb. boned white fish
1 tsp. salt
3 tbsp. flour
2 eggs
4 tbsp. oil

Clean and cut fish into thin slices 2 inches square. Sprinkle with salt, roll in flour, and slightly beaten egg. Fry in a small amount of oil until brown on both sides and tender. Serve with vinegar-soy sauce (see recipe on page 12).

FISH FRIED IN DEEP FAT

(Tang Soo Au)

1 white fish (3 lbs.)	2 tbsp. vinegar
½ cup soy sauce	2 cups oil

Wash and clean fish. Leave the head on, if desired. Slash across the fish every inch on both sides. Combine the soy sauce and vinegar and pour over the fish. Let stand 30 minutes. Fry in deep fat until done, then remove to a meat platter.

Sauce

1½ cups water	2 tbsp. corn starch
2 tbsp. soy sauce	¼ cup mushrooms
½ tbsp. vinegar	¼ cup lotus roots
6 tbsp. sugar	¼ cup carrot

To the water add soy sauce, vinegar, and sugar. Heat. Mix corn starch with a little water and add, stirring constantly until sauce thickens. Cut the mushrooms, lotus roots and carrots into attractive pieces and add to the sauce. Cook for 10 minutes slowly and pour over the fish. Bamboo shoots may be added, if desired.

RAW OYSTERS

(Kool-hoi)

1 pint oysters

Pick over oysters and remove any shell. Arrange attractively on green leaves and serve with vinegar-soy sauce (see recipe page 12). Clams may be prepared and served in the same way.

DESSERTS

As food passes round it grows less. But with words, the further they go, the more they increase. (KOREAN PROVERB)

The favorite dessert in Korea is fresh fruit. There is always some kind of fresh fruit in season the year round. Peculiar to Korea are the delicious persimmons that ripen in the fall, the Korean pear which is a firm, sweet, juicy fruit, and the Korean date.

CINNAMON FOLDS

(Mils-sam)

1 cup flour	1 tsp. cinnamon
¾ tsp. salt	1 tbsp. sugar
1 tsp. baking powder	parsley, spinach or
¾ to 1 cup water	celery leaves
2 tbsp. prepared sesame	3 tbsp. oil
seed (see recipe p. 11)	

Mix flour, salt, and baking powder together. Add enough water to make a thin batter. Combine prepared sesame seed, cinnamon and sugar. Mix well. Fry the batter in a small amount of fat in pieces 3 inches long and 2 inches wide. While frying the batter place one leaf on the upper side of the batter, then turn over. Place 1 tsp. of the cinnamon mixture on the side now in view and fold batter in half to enclose cinnamon. Press edges together. The leaf should be on the outside. Serve hot or cold.

DATE BALLS

(Cho-raan)

30 dates	1 tsp. cinnamon
2 tbsp. sugar	3 tbsp. pine nuts

Seed dates and steam for 15 minutes. Run through a very coarse strainer. Add the sugar and cinnamon. Mix well. Make into balls ½ inch in diameter and roll in finely chopped pine nuts. Arrange attractively on small plates.

CHESTNUTS

(Sang-newl)

Remove the shells from raw chestnuts and cut flat across the top and bottom. Cut the sides of the chestnuts into diamond shapes. Put into sweetened water until time to serve. Arrange attractively on small plates.

CHESTNUT BALLS
(You-raan)

30 chestnuts	2 tsp. cinnamon
5 tbsp. sugar	4 tbsp. pine nuts

Boil, the chestnuts in the shells 10–15 minutes. Remove shells and skin. Mash. Add sugar and cinnamon. Mix well. When the mixture sticks together, make into balls ½ inch in diameter and roll in finely chopped pine nuts. If the nuts do not stick well, first roll the chestnut balls in a little honey and then in the nuts.

FLOWER CAKES
(Hwa-juhn)

1 cup flour	1/3 cup water
½ tsp. salt	5 dates
2 tbsp. sugar	parsley or celery leaves
1 tsp. baking powder	3 tbsp. oil

Mix flour, salt, sugar, and baking powder. Add enough water to make a stiff dough and roll it to a ⅛-inch thickness. Cut in circles 1½ inches in diameter. Decorate each circle with bits of shredded date and leaves pressed flat in the dough. Fry on both sides in a small amount of fat.

STRAWBERRY PUNCH
(Dal-ke hwa chyah)

12 large strawberries	4 cups water
1 cup sugar	2 tbsp. pine nuts

Wash berries and remove stems. Slice and add 1 cup sugar. Boil water and remaining sugar for 5 minutes and cool. Place berries in small glass bowls. Add the sugar syrup and a few pine nuts to each bowl. Serve with a spoon.

GINGER TEA

(Sang-cha)

- 1/3 cup sliced ginger root
- 5 cups water
- 2 dates
- 3 walnuts
- 1 tbsp. pine nuts
- ¾ cups sugar
- ½ tsp. cinnamon

Wash, scrape and slice ginger in very thin slices. Add water and boil for 20 minutes. Remove the ginger. Slice dates in thin slices. Shell and blanch walnut meats and cut in small pieces. Remove the brown covering from the pine nuts. Add sugar and cinnamon to the water in which the ginger was cooked While still hot, serve in cups, adding a small amount of pine nuts, walnuts and dates to each cup.

FRUIT PUNCH

(Hwa chyah)

- 1 grapefruit
- 1 cup sugar
- 6 cups water
- 3 tbsp. pine nuts
- fresh or candied cherries

Cut grapefruit into halves and remove all the pulp. Add ¼ cup of sugar to pulp and let stand 30 minutes. Boil ¾ cup sugar with the water and cool. Put a spoonful of grapefruit pulp in each of six small individual glass bowls. Add 1 cup of the sugar and water. Sprinkle pine nuts on top. Add 6 or 8 fresh cherries, or 2 or 3 candied cherries, to each bowl. Serve with a spoon.

FRIED HONEY CAKES

(Yak-kwa)

Sugar Syrup (A)	Sugar Syrup (B)
¾ cup sugar	2 cups sugar
¾ cup water	2 cups water
1 tsp. honey	1 tsp. flavoring

5 cups flour
½ cup oil
oil for deep fat frying
½ cup pine nuts

Sugar Syrup (A)

Boil sugar and water for 1 minute. Remove from the fire. Add honey and set aside to cool.

Sugar Syrup (B)

Boil sugar and water for 5 minutes. Remove from fire and add flavoring. (Juice extracted from freshly chopped ginger root is a desirable flavoring, and is added 1 minute before removing syrup from the fire.) Cool.

Put flour in a mixing bowl. Hollow out the center by pushing the flour to the sides of the bowl. Pour in oil and the ¾ cup of sugar syrup (A). Mix the oil and syrup rapidly, gradually incorporating a little flour until all the flour is mixed in well. Press mixture together with the hands to make it adhere. Divide into 50 small balls using 1 heaping tablespoon to make each ball. Press each ball into a circle ¼ inch thick, or press the mixture into an oblong shape ¼ inch thick and cut into 2-inch squares. Before frying, press each cake firmly together to prevent edges from crumbling.

Heat oil to 375 degrees F. Add a few cakes at a time and fry, turning often. When a light brown color, remove from the oil and put into the 2 cups of sugar syrup (B).

Leave 2-3 minutes. Remove from the syrup and sprinkle the tops with pine nuts that have been chopped fine. If desired, cinnamon can also be sprinkled on top.

CANDIED RAISINS AND PINE NUTS
(Kun-po-do chot juhn-kwa)

2 tbsp. water
5 tbsp. sugar
½ cup raisins
½ cup pine nuts
pine needles

Put raisins and pine nuts on the tips of pine needles (one to each needle). Tie four or five needles together at the opposite ends of the needle points. Boil water and sugar slowly until a syrup forms. Dip the raisins and pine nuts in the syrup. Let cool. Arrange candied ginger, raisins, and pine nuts attractively on a small plate.

CANDIED GINGER
(Sang juhn kwa)

1 cup sliced ginger
½ cup sugar
3 tbsp. water

Wash, scrape, and slice ginger in very thin pieces. Cover with water and boil 5 minutes. Drain. Again cover with water and boil 5 minutes. Drain.

Boil sugar and water slowly until a syrup forms. Add ginger and cook slowly until the syrup is all absorbed and the ginger is dry and sugar coated.

A majestic view has no charm when the table is bare. (KOREAN PROVERB)

The Korean menu is thought of in terms of the number of dishes prepared. For the simple family meal the number is 3 or 4, but when guests are invited, it is 10 or 12 or more according to the importance of the dinner. Guests are supposed to sample all the different dishes. The basic foods in the menus are rice, soup, and *keem-chee*.

SPRING MENUS

Luncheon

White rice (*Heen pahb*)
Vegetable soup (*Cha-soh kook*)
Bean sprouts (*Khong na-mool*)
Salted beef (*Jahng jo-rim*)
Spring keem-chee (*Pom Keem-chee*)

Dinner

Rice and beans (*Pah pahb*)
Spinach soup (*See-kum-che kook*)
Lettuce salad (*Sang-chee na-mool*)
Field potato, carrot, onion (*Cha-soh juhn*)
Broiled tongue (*Oo-sul kui*)
Salted fish (*Sang-suhn jo-rim*)
Spring keem-chee (*Pom keem-chee*)
Fresh fruit

Dinner

White rice (*Heen pahb*)
Beef ball soup (*Wan-ja kook*)
Spinach (*See-kum-chee na-mool*)
Bean sprouts (*Khong na-mool*)
Mushrooms and beef (*Song-i jim*)
Broiled beef (*Ko-kee jim*)
Spring keem-chee (*Pom keem-chee*)
Fresh fruit

Luncheon

White rice (*Heen pahb*)
Cabbage soup (*Paj-hoo kook*)
Fried squash (*Ho-pahb juhn*)
Turnip-beef salad (*Moo sang-cha*)
Turnip keem-chee (*Moo keem-chee*)

Dinner

Rice and green peas (*Kong pahb*)
Sesame seed soup (*Cho-kay tang*)
Fried green peppers (*Ko-chooh juhn*)
Vegetable-pork salad (*Chai-yuk sang cha*)
Chicken with vegetables (*Tahk jim*)
Salted beef squares (*Jahng jo-rim*)
Cucumber keem-chee (*O-i keem-chee*)
Fruit punch (*Hwa chyah*)

Dinner

White rice (*Heen pahb*)
Cucumber soup (*O-i kook*)
Fried egg plant (*Kah-ri juhn*)
Beef and vegetables cooked at the table (*Juhn-kol*)
Carrot, turnip, cucumber salad (*Tang-kun na-mool*)
Cucumber keem-chee (*O-i keem-chee*)
Fruit punch (*Hwa chyah*)

Luncheon

Rice and beans (*Pah pahb*)
Cabbage soup (*Paj-hoo kook*)
Carrot and turnip salad (*Moo sang-cha*)
Fried egg plant (*Kah-ri juhn*)
Salted beef squares (*Jang-san juhk*)
Cucumber keem-chee (*O-i keem-chee*)

Dinner

Rice and mushrooms (*Song-i pahb*)
Egg soup (*Ke-ran kook*)
Spinach (*See-kum-chee na-mool*)
Fried squash (*Ho-pahk juhn*)
Turnips and beef (*Moo-sook-jang-ah-gee*)
Broiled pork (*Ton-yuk kui*)
Turnip keem-chee (*Mu keem-chee*)
Fresh fruit

Dinner

White rice (*Heen pahb*)
Egg plant soup (*Ka-gi kook*)
Carrot, turnip, cucumber salad (*Tang-kun na-mool*)
Meat, vegetables with vermicelli (*Chop-chai*)
Beef and onions on skewers (*Pah sahn-juhk*)
Cucumber keem-chee (*O-i keem-chee*)
Fresh fruit

WINTER MENUS

Luncheon

Rice and potatoes (*Kahm-cha pahb*)
Bean sprout soup (*Khong na-mool kook*)
Cucumbers with beef (*O-i jim*)
Fried liver (*Kahn juhn*)
Winter keem-chee (*Tong keem-chee*)

Dinner

Rice and sweet potatoes (*Ko-koo-mah pahb*)
Beef and turnip soup (*Ko-oum kook*)
Bean sprouts (*Khong na-mool*)
Fried spinach (*See-kum-chee juhn*)
Chicken "pok-kum" (*Tahn pok-kum*)
Boiled pork (*Oo-yuk puen-yuk*)
Winter keem-chee (*Tong keem-chee*)
Fresh fruit

Special Dinner

White rice (*Heen pahb*)
Meat dumplings (*Man-tu*)
Spinach (*See-kum-chee na-mool*)
Fried peppers (*Ko-chooh juhn*)
Egg folds (*Als-sam*)
Mushrooms with beef (*Song-i jim*)
Fried oysters (*Kool juhn*)
Broiled pheasant (*Gooung kui*)
Winter keem-chee (*Tong keem-chee*)
Chestnut Balls (*You-raan*)
Date balls (*Cho-raan*)
Fresh fruit